Biologists often begin  rocks, chasing critters through their scientific training, many quit looking at animals, they move up. Not so George James Kenagy, who has maintained his fascination with whole organisms, the communities they form, and the landscapes they inhabit. In his lively company, you can observe geckos, beavers, pandas, ants, kangaroo rats, desert iguanas, snowy egrets, deer mice, surf smelt, spiny lobsters, ground squirrels, darkling beetles, western rattlesnakes, hoary marmots, and other marvels of the living world. One of the most interesting animals you'll meet in these pages is the author himself.
—SCOTT RUSSELL SANDERS
    author of *Earth Works: Selected Essays*

The great joy in reading Kenagy's *Everyday Creatures* is seeing nature through the eyes of a sensitive scientist, trained to notice and record the smallest elements and changes in animals and their environments. Drawing from a lifetime of experience with lizards and pandas and kangaroo rats, the author conveys both intriguing facts and acute observations. His keen fascination with the natural world will make you want to pay more attention to the wonders around you.
—MICHAEL N. MCGREGOR
    author of *Pure Act: The Uncommon Life of Robert Lax*

With a child's enthusiasm and a scientist's acumen, Professor Kenagy takes us to his favorite haunts to share with us his intimate knowledge of nature. To read *Everyday Creatures* is to be swept away on an extended field trip with a keen naturalist guide. We come to appreciate the subtle doings of rivers, forests, deserts, and shrublands as we learn about all manner of life from kangaroo rats and giant pandas to beetles, beavers, and smelt.
—JOHN MARZLUFF
    author of *Welcome to Subirdia* and *Gifts of the Crow*

"And gladly would he learn, and gladly teach." This description of the Nun's Priest in Chaucer's Canterbury Tales was recalled for me by George James Kenagy's voice in *Everyday Creatures*. Several of the essays in this collection evoke the author's early explorations of southern California's desert through which he discovered his vocation as a biologist. Within these and the other stories in this fine collection, though, Kenagy also offers a lifetime of insights, gleaned from his distinguished career as a teacher and researcher at the University of Washington.

—JOHN ELDER
co-editor of *The Norton Book of Nature Writing*

Everyday Creatures is a story of discovery, told with precision, intimacy, and wonder. Kenagy's prose is clean and entirely accessible, informative to the scientist and non-scientist alike, a testament to a lifetime of attentiveness to the natural world.

—GREGORY MARTIN
author of *Mountain City* and *Stories for Boys*

Kenagy is a rare specimen among modern biologists: a true naturalist, with deep knowledge of an astonishing variety of plants and animals. This book takes you from China to New England, from eastern Washington State to western Sonora, Mexico, with rewarding stops in between, all steeped in the decades of field work that have allowed him to contribute so much to our knowledge of the natural world. To read this is to be taken to all these places, and to learn about such diverse things as the temperatures that make beetles happy, ground squirrels that prey on chipmunks, the surprising adaptations of kangaroo rats, and even the relationship between campus committees and Canada geese. I read it from beginning to end without putting it down, and suspect you will too.

—DONALD K. GRAYSON
author of *The Great Basin: A Natural Prehistory*

EVERYDAY CREATURES

EVERYDAY CREATURES

A Naturalist on the Surprising Beauty
of Ordinary Life in Wild Places

GEORGE JAMES KENAGY

Copyright © 2018 George James Kenagy

Library of Congress Cataloging-in-Publication Data
Kenagy, George James

Everyday creatures: a naturalist on the surprising beauty of
ordinary life in wild places

Subjects: Nature, Natural History, Deserts

Cover and book design: Mary Kenagy Mitchell
Illustrations: Nancy J. Smith

ISBN 978-0692056448

Cover photo: eastern Sierra Nevada from California's Owens
Valley, courtesy of Getty Images

Permission to quote from E.O. Wilson's
Biophilia granted by Harvard University Press

DOCKSIDE SAILING PRESS ™
www.docksidesailingpress.com
Newport Beach, California

For
Joshua, Juliana,
Ernie, and Felix

Contents

Prologue 1

1. Secrets of Spiny Saltbush 7

2. Acquaintance with Ants 23

3. Taking a Walk with a Beaver 33

4. Lone Egret in a Lagoon 45

5. Smelt Mating on a Beach 51

6. Gecko Ambush 59

7. Someone Who Showed Me 65

8. Meeting Kangaroo Rats and Deserts 81

9. Underground Mysteries of Kangaroo Rats 113

10. Meeting the Beetles 133

11. The Panda's Message 167

12. Ground Squirrel Who Ate Chipmunks 183

13. Caught in the Act 199

Epilogue 209

References and Further Reading 213

Acknowledgments 217

PROLOGUE

FINDING WILD PLACES

A few years ago I wrote down a list of places where I have experienced personal connections with nature. Each name on the list called out to me with memories. I decided it would be fun to write some stories about these places and the creatures that inhabit them—stories that would be more personal than the scientific papers I was used to publishing as a college professor.

I've found that long-term immersion in a place where I've studied a population of animals creates a deep attachment to the landscape—to everything, not just the animals. As a scientist, I've logged thousands of hours observing, measuring, capturing, handling, and releasing animals back into the wild. These experiences all yielded data that I used in my research. But the landscapes, plants, and animals have remained deeply and personally in my memory, a part of me.

I was a college sophomore in the mid 1960s when my parents acquired a small property in California's dry Owens Valley, on the eastward back of the Sierra Nevada. The little house sat along a creek that brought precious water down from the Sierra into the valley. Mountains towered ten thousand feet on either side of a valley floor that measured only a few miles wide. I peered upward to glistening granite peaks that held North America's southernmost active glaciers, icy and dirty white in summer, a contrast to the blazing heat in the valley below. In winter the valley would be covered with white and cold. The big river in the valley bottom quietly carried the waters from the Sierra southward toward the Mojave Desert.

The Owens Valley I found then, at age nineteen, would become an important place for me, a retreat. My attachment to that landscape developed during years that were formative both personally and professionally. After graduating with a degree in zoology, I entered a PhD program in ecology, which I believed would allow me to plumb the heights and depths of nature through scientific inquiry. Surely, I expected, science would offer a way to understand the pristine natural world. How could small mammals that find shelter in underground burrows survive and reproduce in the desert floor of the Owens Valley, with its frozen soil surfaces in winter and burning sandy substrate in summer? The modest winter precipitation of this place diminished to drought by late spring. From the first, I loved the spare and extreme feel of this place, its sandy soils, rocks, and wind. The smells of dry alkali dust and pungent scrub vegetation in the heat of summer remain vividly in my mind.

I was twenty-two when I began my graduate studies, the same age as Charles Darwin in 1831, when he joined Captain Robert FitzRoy's voyage to chart the navigability of South America's shores aboard *HMS Beagle*. Richard Henry Dana was about the same age in 1834, when he dropped out of college to sail from Boston aboard the *Pilgrim* around South America to the shores of Mexico's northern territory known as Alta California. And here I was, in California, ready to explore. What would my experience in nature be, as I attempted to launch my PhD dissertation in the Owens Valley?

I was offered a teaching assistantship in the ecology course. I confidently told my parents what ecology was. When my mother told her mother I would be teaching ecology, my grandmother's delight was enormous—the delight of a woman whose education ended with elementary school, when she was conscripted, as the oldest daughter, to help on the family farm. Now she was thrilled to learn from me a new word, "ecology." Actually I didn't yet know what ecology meant in the academic research world, but I was charmed by the word, by the professors, and by the first Earth Day in 1970.

I first experienced nature as a youngster in central Oregon's high desert of sagebrush and juniper, and in the adjoining Cascade Mountains, with their volcanic peaks, forests, lakes, and streams. Led by my parents, neither of whom had completed college, our family camped, fished, and hiked. We lived with farm animals on small acreages. My mother's father was a dairy farmer, who understood the lives of his Jersey cows, some of whom I still recall by name. My father's dad hunted in Oregon's wild forests. As I grew, I began to experience nature on my own. Ecology was all of this outdoor stuff: fresh air, rocks, bushes, trees, and animals inhabiting their spaces. The key, I felt, was just to go out to the places where nature was happening.

In my later youth I met southern California's coastal scrub, chaparral, and San Gabriel Mountains, then the Mojave Desert and the great Sierra Nevada. My years as an undergraduate and graduate student continued in the environmental wonderland of California and the neighboring Sonoran Desert and Great Basin Desert. As a graduate student I also experienced the tropics, first in Costa Rica and then in South America, where I also made a pilgrimage out to the Galapagos.

During my professional life I returned to the Pacific Northwest, to Washington, where my home became the cool forests, the Olympic and Cascade Mountains, and the drier ponderosa forests and sagebrush-steppe of the eastern part of the state. During these years I also became at home, at least temporarily, in some of Earth's other continental treasures: the European Alps, Australia's eastern forests and arid outback, Mexico's deserts and central highlands and Yucatan, and South America's dry Mediterranean matorral and the cool forests and pampas of Patagonia, and finally in Asia, in the forest of China's Hengduan Mountain region.

Recently I've begun to wonder if attraction to the complexities of modern biology is leading scientists away from opportunities to experience and discover nature's truths. I'm thinking of all the genetics and DNA sequencing, all the theoretical population modeling, and all the science-as-usual attention to testing abstract theory, as promising and significant as those dimensions of science may remain. I am also concerned about the great attraction to telling the stories of endangered species, as important as that will continue to be, because it results in such a strong shift of creative energy into socio-political advocacy, which we also need.

I believe that the character of wild places — simply the stories of the rocks, soil, water, plants, and animals going about their everyday business — represents the ultimate truth of nature. I think that I came to this belief early, as I immersed myself in wild places as a graduate student. Although I enthusiastically became an academic scientist, perhaps my most recent sentiments about the value of nature's truths confirm that I was cut out to be a naturalist first.

As I wrote the essays assembled in this book, it became clear to me that I have developed rich attachments to nature when I invested a great deal of time in a particular place. But I also realized that I have found connection even in short moments, as long as I was paying attention.

Some of my most meaningful experiences and best memories have come from observations of animal behavior that happened in only brief moments. When this occurred, the place became just as memorable as the event itself. On the whimsical side, my first observation of golden-mantled ground squirrel mating behavior, during a long series of years studying a population in eastern Washington's ponderosa forest, did not result from patiently waiting behind a blind or quietly stalking a patrolling male who was monitoring all the females in the forest. The copulating squirrels simply appeared, in the middle of their act, on top of a tree stump right behind me and my family as we were gathering fire wood on a leisurely morning in the forest near my study area.

I have come to love what I think of as *moments in nature*. They are a distillation of everything important and delightful in the grandeur of nature. They are place. They are time. They capture it all. Sometimes they happen in a place I know deeply and well, and sometimes they occur in a place where I have been only once, as an element of surprise — just a *moment in nature.*

At these times, I feel rewarded simply for being there and paying attention. Perhaps I'm witnessing a truly rare event in the life of an animal or an ecosystem, or maybe it's just common, everyday behavior in a context made special because I catch the moment. The stories I've collected for this little book tell about my personal connections with places, with *moments in nature*, and with everyday creatures.

1

SECRETS OF SPINY SALTBUSH

SEEKING NATURE'S WAY

I am standing in a place of hard physical conditions, a landscape of stony and sandy soils eroded down through washes and across alluvial fans from nearby mountains, down to a dry valley floor where salts become concentrated to form a dusty alkaline substrate. Rugged and small perennial bushes, widely spaced, grow out of this soil. Delicate annual herbs appear from time to time, after it rains, usually in small numbers and rarely in dense blankets—some years not at all. Mysterious critters, hidden from my senses most of the time, inhabit this desert place: coyotes, kangaroo rats, whiptail lizards, sidewinders, shrikes, black-throated sparrows, darkling beetles, blister beetles, scorpions, spiders, ants. I am pleased to meet them when we coincide, giving me the privilege to observe their private lives.

As an ecology graduate student in the late 1960s I wondered if I could find something new in nature, out on a dusty plot in this arid scrub. Ecologists look for connections linking organisms that share a place and make up an ecological community. I wondered if I could uncover pieces of the puzzle that reflect these connections. I have continued to wonder about finding science that is true to nature throughout my life as a professional biologist.

The saltbush scrub habitat I chose for my research project showed no signs of human presence other than my own, and that exclusiveness attracted me. Being surrounded by pristine desert heightened my hope for discovery. Over the three years of my project, the solitude of this place, the Owens Valley, always awaited my monthly visits, at a distant five-hour drive from Los Angeles. A remarkable trough nearly 10,000 feet deep, the valley dropped down between two uplifted crests: the Sierra Nevada to the west and the White and Inyo Ranges to the east. This profound groove in Earth, only a few miles wide, amounts to a northward finger of the Mojave Desert, pointing onward to the Great Basin of Nevada. The farther you follow that finger, the more uplifted mountains and intervening north-south troughs you find. Out on the edge of this expansive, quiet North American interior, I was attempting to formulate a project to meet the requirements for a PhD, the basis for getting a job as a university professor. I didn't really know what that meant, but I expected it would require a lot of work, both physical and mental. I felt encouragement when I was out there alone, surrounded by trustworthy nature. I met biologists who expressed their love of nature. I met others whose science puzzled me and seemed too simple, or too complex. I chose this particular place in the desert because I believed it must hold nature's truths.

The dominant shrub in this plant association, spiny saltbush (Latin species designation *Atriplex confertifolia*), gives the whole biotic community its name: the saltbush scrub or shadscale scrub. Spiny saltbush held a curious attraction for me. Each time I returned I stood among the saltbushes and regained the sense that I was back in a wild and desolate place. I followed the passage of seasons in a series of study plots I laid out. Now it was late winter. The mature bushes seemed like rugged bonsais, only a foot or so high and wide, yet some of them the better part of a century old. The smells of pungent perennial vegetation were telling me that this place was alive and waiting to erupt with a new season of productivity. The small, leathery leaves of spiny saltbush showed a gray to silver sheen, matching the dull glare of the sky that followed yesterday's rain that touched dormant soil. Today's dark sky added to the cold impression of desert winter. Although nighttime air temperatures often fell below freezing, the sun provided perceptible daytime warmth, especially when wind was not blowing. But now, in winter, the tough desert shrubs were operating just above the level of complete dormancy.

Down on the loose soil surface, a few scratchings and tiny footprints indicated that other life goes on year round — kangaroo rats, the most numerous representatives of rodent nightlife here. Also in the soil around the base of shrubs, I spotted tiny bright green shoots of early germinating annuals, pushing up from the suspended life contained in seeds. These dainty herbs — buckwheats, mustards, desert asters, and more — became the temporary companions of the shrubs. The annual herbs would produce their flowers later on, in early springtime. Among other shrubs, greasewood, bud sage, and boxthorn just gave up and shed their leaves for the winter, but spiny saltbush's leaves persisted, perennial. Spiny saltbush regrew new batches of leaves to replace the older leaves, thanks to winter precipitation that restored water to the soil. The sunshine and warmth of early spring would bring on a renewal of life in the ecosystem with full force.

Here and there in western North America's interior the shadscale scrub community appears in patches, typically on stony and alkaline soils, or associated with now-dry lakebeds left over from the melting end of the last ice age. Nevada has the greatest proportion of shadscale scrub of any state. The shadscale's farthest extremes are North Dakota and Chihuahua, Mexico. I became acquainted with this habitat in the Owens Valley, in the transition between the Mojave and Great Basin Deserts. Other species of *Atriplex* saltbush live in alkaline soils around North America where summers become hot and dry. Following my years as a graduate student, I later became acquainted with more *Atriplex* species in deserts of Australia, South America, Africa and Eurasia. Saltbushes have inhabited Earth's deserts since ancient times when today's continents were joined as supercontinents.

As a graduate student I decided to study the community of rodents living in the shadscale scrub because I was fascinated by the behavior and population biology of small mammals. I watched these modest creatures emerge from their burrows at night, after the heat passed, to forage in open spaces and at scattered bushes. I wondered how my observations might explain the variety of species living together.

My parents' small property in California's Owens Valley became my field station as a graduate student. To reach my research site on the remote and drier east side of the valley, I drove across Highway 395, crossed a bridge over the Owens River, and headed into the shadscale. The Owens River meandered quietly through the dry valley floor, bringing waters from the eastern Sierra southward through the desert, where the precious life-giving fluid was captured by a giant aqueduct and delivered to Los Angeles for human consumption. Settlement in the Owens Valley was greatly curtailed beginning in the early twentieth century when the big city bought up land and water rights. This, in fact, promoted the long-term obscurity of the Owens Valley, even as it turned out to protect a valuable ecosystem.

With each monthly progression of the seasons I returned to register changes in the shadscale scrub community — the annual cycle of reproduction, growth, then a long quietness. I loved to walk out there. Each time it was as if it were the first. I staked out individual shrubs of all the common species. Each month I made notes and photographed them. We were now in the midst of spring. This was the same place. But it was different. I noted a light lime-green added to upper twigs of spiny saltbush, an adornment of juicy-looking new leaves more than a centimeter across. I reached down and picked one, rubbed it between my fingers, showing a schmear of green colors. I picked a few more and put them in my mouth — a tiny bite of tasty, somewhat salty spinach. In the coming weeks additional structures of the same soft color grew higher up on the twigs of the female shrubs. These were the two-winged fruiting bracts that develop at the base of the tiny flowers. These bracts hold the seeds. Each adult female plant produces several hundred bracts that mature by late summer.

When I returned in late summer to check my spiny saltbush and the other species, I saw that heat and aridity had taken their toll on water balance. Water is a limiting resource for all organisms here. Leaves of all the shrub species were parched, which means water stress for the plants and for any leaf-eating animal. I sensed that growth rates had ebbed, and this year's new saltbush leaves were now blended in appearance with the old — small and tough. I was also greeted by a new impression—the stunning outcome of this year's productivity, the gorgeous winged fruiting bracts of spiny saltbush that jumped out at me with a shocking crimson, interrupting the drab desert. In my journal pages I also noted bright, straw-yellow margins on the red bracts, which made them stand out even more. The presence of "wings" on the bracts suggests flight. Strong desert winds propel these bracts away from the maternal plant. This mobility helps the seeds, held deep between the two wings, to disperse from where they originated.

Late one summer afternoon, as the sun's intensity subsided and the desert world cooled down from its midday heat, I took a short walk, for fun, to look for signs of daytime animal life. Eventually I was rewarded when whiptails and desert spiny lizards emerged in search of insects and spiders. These reptiles had last been out hunting during the cooler hours of late morning. Even lizards give up during the extreme heat of summer midday in the desert. The presence of small, juvenile lizards among those I spotted was testimony to successful reproduction in response to the springtime pulse of food that allowed hatchlings to get a good start on life. I generally saw whiptail lizards more often than desert spinies, but that may be due to their behavior rather than their population density. The whiptails were more conspicuous because they roved around in search of prey and sometimes made rustling sounds that attracted my attention to the litter beneath shrubs where they cruised for food. Desert spiny lizards sat quietly, in waiting, and ambushed passers by. These are two different ways of making a living, if you're a lizard. Spiny saltbush is just one member of the interlinked community of plant and animal species that succeed in this place.

I continued to witness the passage of seasons in saltbush, adjusting itself from minimal maintenance of lethargic winter leaves to the spring renaissance, and so on. Saltbush's day and night condition also shifted, as with all plants, alternating between daytime photosynthesis and storage of energy, followed by nighttime utilization of energy for maintenance and growth. Plant biologists discovered that spiny saltbush leaves are unusual; they lack the typical photosynthesizing cells lined up just beneath the epidermis cells that cover the upper and lower surfaces. Instead, this saltbush has an even deeper layer of photosynthesizing cells that form a wreath-like circle around the tubing that conducts body fluids and chemicals in and out of the leaves. Deep inside its leaves, spiny saltbush operates with a special version of photosynthesis that runs faster, operates at higher temperatures, and uses less water. This made me wonder how spiny saltbush came to be different.

I watched a specially marked individual spiny saltbush for seven years. The general character and major branches remained the same. Perhaps it had been there for most of a century. The number of leaves, growth of new twigs, and numbers of seed bracts varied each year. Most years I saw no germination of new sprouts from the seed bank. Dense clusters of bracts remained intact beneath some bushes for several years. Nobody knows the fate of all these seeds.

Spiny saltbush manages its balance of water and salts in an exceptional way, compared to standard plant physiology. In drawing water from salty soil, the roots of saltbush pull in the sodium chloride salt pervading the ground water. High salt concentrations could be more toxic for plants under these conditions than for an overdosing human on doctor's orders to adopt a low-sodium diet. After taking on the onerous burden of salt from the soil, instead of excluding it in the first place at the roots through an energy-consuming process, spiny saltbush must get rid of the salt. The surprising answer to "how" is that the outer cells of the leaf actively excrete salt right out onto the leaf's surface. The surface, in turn, is equipped with bladder-like cells that hold the salt in a permanent, densely concentrated reservoir that no longer participates in the plant's metabolism. The concept of coating yourself with a salt cake is unique. It's remarkable that saltbush goes to all this trouble to process something that it didn't need inside in the first place. However, the result is that the salt coating may help to defend spiny saltbush from consumption by vegetarian predators.

In wondering how spiny saltbush came to make a successful living and be numerically dominant here, I imagined that it conquered hardships of heat, aridity, and salt more elaborately than other shrub species faced with salty soils. Spiny saltbush is what ecologists call an indicator species. As a single marker species it indicates a set of conditions that allow a particular community to gather together. The other species have also solved the challenges of living in that environment. Some of the other shrubs in my study area had evocative spiny Latin names: *Menodora spinescens*, *Grayia spinosa*, and *Artemisia spinescens*. Each of these represents a shrub of a different family, so none entered the community by sharing a common ancestor. Prickly twigs and thorns and leaves are a common solution for curbing decimation by herbivores.

It was good to be out in the shadscale again in the heat of summer—another evening in the desert where I belonged with my rodents. No moon, only the gentlest, light breeze. Quiet. Suddenly, piercing coyote yips and squeals raised goose bumps that chilled my neck and arms. A conversation erupted between two groups who howled to inform one another of their whereabouts.

The first few kangaroo rats were beginning to emerge from their burrows. Kangaroo rats are easy to watch in the twilight if you remain still and just look around. First they walk slowly on all fours, adjusting to above-ground conditions as they emerge from their burrows and begin to explore. When commuting to a nearby foraging spot, they fire off at rapid pace, hopping kangaroo-style on just the two extra-long hind feet and using the long, rigidly held tail as a counterbalance. I have clocked them at up to 20 miles an hour. Tiny pocket mice are out and about too, but they hunker down, under and near bushes, and can't be seen so readily. All across North America's deserts, various nocturnal rodent citizens of the wild are participating in this nightlife, combing their way through the seed bank in the sandy soil. One of the theories of how different seed-eating rodent species can fit together in an ecological community is that the bigger species specialize on finding bigger seeds and the smaller rodent species go around finding smaller seeds, dividing up nature's resources. In tonight's dim, natural skylight I watch and patrol as I move through my trapping routine. I can see the glaciers atop the Sierra Nevada, dimly lit by the night sky. Another surprise: wing beats and then the silhouette of a swooping barn owl. So much life fills this place at night. I think the night is mysterious because it's not what we think of as our time.

The kangaroo rats and pocket mice remain underground all day and come out onto the surface only at intervals during the night. To monitor their body condition, weight, and reproductive status, I capture them in small sheet-aluminum box traps. In winter I include a cotton ball they use for comfort and insulation. The rodents readily enter these traps, baited with a small seed reward. Over the months the same individuals return, creating a personal history of growth, seasonally fluctuating weight, reproduction, and then finally, if they disappear from the data collection, I may assume they have fallen prey to one of their predators: owls, snakes, mammalian carnivores such as coyotes or badgers.

To facilitate my tasks, I carry a red plastic bucket (claimed from a give-away pile at the zoology department stock room) to hold notebook, clipboard, datasheets, pencils, flashlight, and a scale for weighing the animals. The bucket gradually takes on a supply of sand, leaves, spiders, whatever falls into it during the night, including seeds and rodent droppings that fall from the traps when I open them to examine each animal. As I walk around I prefer to avoid using my flashlight, except when examining an animal held in my hand, which requires close-up attention. My eyes seem to accustom to the night sky, moon or not, and the ground is fairly light in tone. In fact a full moon, to me, becomes almost blinding. There is much to hear. Coyote howls are the loudest sounds. The rats and mice make gentle swooshes as they kick sand or run across the alkaline soil. Their rare growls or squeaks have a low-level impact on my ear, but rodents also produce ultrasonic emissions of which I am never aware as I pause and listen to silence.

I lift each trap with a closed door from the desert floor and immediately discern by weight a kangaroo rat (heavy) or pocket mouse (light). I hear tiny scratchings made by the creature inside. I particularly love to explore with my hand, which extends gently and eagerly into the trap. I feel a warm ball of fur with tickly, moving feet and claws, and then my fingers draw the animal to the palm of my hand. Nibbling incisors rarely inflict harm to my fingers. I know these little animals have not previously experienced anything as strange as the gentle hand of a curious scientist. I remove the animal and hold its nape, feet, and tail carefully with my left hand. I can make notes on my clipboard as I hold the animal, or I can remember the observation and write after I let the animal go on its way.

Two species of kangaroo rats, very similar in appearance, lived in my study area. All of the twenty-some species of kangaroo rats, found only in North America, belong to the genus *Dipodomys*. This means "two-footed mouse," referring to their kangaroo style of hopping. Merriam's kangaroo rat (*Dipodomys merriami*) was well known to biologists because it is widely distributed throughout North America's deserts. The other species on my research grids, not much studied, was the Great Basin or chisel-toothed kangaroo rat (*Dipodomys microps*).

To learn everything I wanted to find out, I had to do more than trapping. What about the underground burrows? What kinds of nests might they construct in winter to provide insulation for conserving the energy required to maintain body heat? In a nearby area away from my trapping grids I planned to dig down and dissect some burrow systems in order to find out what was going on. These burrow systems certainly had more to tell about the lives of the rodents.

It was winter. I took my shovel and dug into the soft, moist, sandy soil to excavate the nests of chisel-toothed kangaroo rats. A strange plant material—not appearing like any plant I knew here—showed up beneath the fragrant, grassy nests of chisel-tooths. The material appeared fresh and smelled good to me. It looked processed. Was it fermenting? It would take a while to piece together this puzzle. The stuff partly resembled leaves of spiny saltbush, but it partly looked yellowish-chartreuse. Later, after I made microscope slides of the strange material, I looked into the scope and saw that the pieces of the strange material were made up of only the surface part of the leaves of spiny saltbush. But to move more quickly toward answering the puzzle, while still out in the field, I employed some chisel-toothed kangaroo rats that I captured nearby and held in cages for a few days.

I tossed a few leathery saltbush leaves into the cages of my temporary captives. A rat picked up a single leaf with its tiny front paws and brought it to its mouth. It seemed to fiddle around in some way with the leaf, which I could not fully see. I needed to watch up close, from beneath. The answer was an aquarium, mounted above a mirror oriented at 45 degrees on a wooden stand that I fashioned. Staring into the mirror, I watched in awe at what each chisel-toothed kangaroo rat, in turn, was doing. Holding a single leaf with both tiny hands, it wiggled the leaf around at the gape of its mouth, drawing the flat leaf surface over the two chisel-shaped lower incisors. Tiny pieces of debris were falling away, shavings. One side of each shaving had the color and texture of the natural leaf surface; the other side was the bright chartreuse I had seen in the massive deposits in the burrows. Continuing, the rat flipped the leaf and repeated the shaving procedure on the other leaf surface; then it popped the remainder into its mouth, chewed, and swallowed. It took about 20 seconds to shave and consume one leaf; that's three leaves per minute. What an incredible stunt! By shaving the epidermis off both sides, the rats removed a highly concentrated layer of poisonous salts, which were, for the plant, a waste-dump of toxic materials that served to defend the leaf from other herbivores. The rats were consuming only the inner, juicy, starch-loaded tissue.

I worked for a couple more months to uncover more details. I used some captured chisel-tooths again to prepare the shavings for chemical analysis. The salt concentration of the discarded epidermis and bladder cells was 30 times that of salt in the interior. Without supplemental drinking water (which is not available to the small animals in this habitat), consuming the superficial leaf residue would be lethal. Kangaroo rat species in general are well known to be dietary specialists on seeds. My discovery showed that the chisel-tooth has opted out of that tradition for an alternative specialty as a leaf connoisseur.

I wondered how the elaborate process of shaving off leaves became incorporated into the behavior of this rat. Evolutionary theorists recognize that behavior is flexible, especially in mammals, and it can evolve over multiple generations of gradually changed individuals. Inherited, changed behavior can, in turn, promote evolution of changes in structure. In response to the modified behavior of the kangaroo rat, an anatomical change was apparent in the common name given to the animal, chisel-tooth. It amused me that biologists who surveyed the Great Basin and named this rat, noticed that its two lower incisor teeth were broad and flat in front, and chisel-shaped—unlike the narrow, rounded incisors of all the other, seed-eating kangaroo rat species. However, the original namers apparently didn't know how these chisels were used. To them, it was just another descriptive feature of anatomy to help biologists distinguish one species from another. I wondered if the namers had been curious enough to ask why *Dipodomys microps* might have unique lower incisors.

All of what I discovered, as elaborate and beautiful as it seemed to me, was simply ordinary feeding behavior for one particular desert rodent. The fact remains, though, that chisel-tooth's distinctive, alternative lifestyle among kangaroo rats utterly charmed me. Its way of winnowing out harmful elements in its diet and the economy of using only what was needed led to the remarkable bond that formed between kangaroo rat and bush. This connection developed long ago when the evolutionary trajectories of the two organisms intersected, two species that belonged to vastly different lineages, plant and animal, angiosperm and mammal. Their lineages, moving independently through evolutionary time, followed the strict rules of natural selection. Then they met and formed an ecological connection, members of a new alliance.

Through serendipity, my own efforts as a naturalist resulted in an unanticipated observation, something that no human may have previously imagined. A single rodent species member of the shadscale community had seemingly cracked spiny saltbush's secret code. I was thrilled to uncover this bond of ecological community between rodent and shrub. But wasn't the original natural discovery of saltbush's secret by an ancestral chisel-tooth more significant and impressive in the history of life on Earth than what a young ecologist discovered when he wandered out into the desert in the twentieth century? I was simply fortunate to witness and be illuminated by nature's beauty that already existed.

When I discovered the intimate connection between spiny saltbush and chisel-toothed kangaroo rat, I was inclined to think of it as a bond—perhaps because of the fondness suggested by the word itself. Biologists would not ordinarily use the word bond to talk about a relationship between an animal and its food. The word is typically reserved for relationships between individuals of the same species, for example, siblings enjoying the common bond of their family's parentage, or the pair bond of a mated female and male. The bond that I imagined between chisel-tooth and saltbush was an ecological bond, activated by the behavior of animal toward plant. As the bond continued to develop over many seasons and generations, spiny saltbush gave chisel-toothed kangaroo rat its new teeth.

The thick old branches of spiny saltbush are weathered, gray, rough, bleached by sun. Yet new leaves reappear, almost every year, and a few flowers, a few seeds, adorned by red bracts. Saltbush will continue to sustain itself and will provide, despite protection with spines and salt, substance for others in its community. Perhaps no exploiter has cracked the secret code of spiny saltbush as handsomely as chisel-toothed kangaroo rat. But others in the community depend on saltbush as well. Redistributing saltbush's personal biomass back into the ecosystem is an inevitable part of the cycle. Some of saltbush goes back by way of other plant consumers, as small as the little green caterpillars in spring who take their bits. Finally, saltbush goes back into the soil with the decomposition of dead leaves, bracts, and whole bushes. These are the cycles of individual organisms over their lifetimes that form the cycle of ecosystem life.

The delight of discovering the connection between

chisel-toothed kangaroo rat and spiny saltbush has remained with me throughout my life as a professional biologist. I happily recall, as if it were happening again at this moment, finding the strange silver and chartreuse plant material beneath the winter nest in a kangaroo rat burrow, watching the first kangaroo rat as it took a leaf in its paws and held it to its lower incisors, understanding the anatomy of saltbush leaves, and recognizing the function of the mysterious chisel-shaped teeth. By allowing the rat and the bush to teach me their secrets, I somehow felt myself akin to their community.

This highly memorable discovery became a vivid landmark in my scientific career. I see it as a truth of nature. It opened me to the joy that would come with future discoveries, and to a deeper possibility for finding personal and ethical affiliations with whatever new landscapes I might encounter and the creatures I would find in them.

2

ACQUAINTANCE WITH ANTS

Having arrived for a retreat in the quiet beauty of northern New Mexico's vast pinyon-juniper woodland, I was going to have some free time to sneak away and explore on my own. The world of pinyon pines and juniper trees is home to many ant species. Millions and billions of ants who belong to dozens of species prosper in this setting. I knew little about them, but I wanted to get out just to see what they might tell me about themselves. I never had the pet ant farm as a kid, but I've always had a curiosity about ants, just to walk up and watch them, so busy. What were they doing? I wanted to find them in the wild places where they live.

My plan was to find an ant mound and take a personal look at what goes on down at the small scale of ant life. With a small backpack containing field supplies and water, I headed out on this August afternoon from the retreat center and quickly found myself isolated among handsome and healthy pinyons and junipers. Where these two kinds of trees live together across intermediate elevation desert and montane topographies in the American southwest, usually only one species of pinyon tree coexists with one species of juniper, but all in great numbers and over miles and miles of western landscape set on stony and typically red-hued, fairly barren soils. The roundish trees of both species here were bushy as youngsters, but the bigger and older individuals also retained mostly rotund globular shapes. Great openings remained on the ground among the trees of this sparse desert land, and I loved this particular woodland because that open space invited you to come inside.

Thinking of the acquaintance I was hoping to make with ants here in New Mexico, I recalled an earlier adventure as a graduate student—a connection with ants. On a weekend class field trip, my herpetology professor commissioned us to get close to nature by paying attention to lizards out in a wild piece of California oak scrubland. He dispatched us for an hour of personal quiet time with orders to watch an individual lizard as long as possible and to write down everything it did. Fun. I quickly found a coast horned lizard (a.k.a. horny toad) on sandy soil in an open space, and soon thereafter I spotted a nearby ant mound. Taking up a comfortable observation station and fixing my binoculars to my eyes, I sat quietly. The lizard had initially been startled by my approach and darted a short distance away, but now it resumed what appeared to be its normal morning activity. Shortly I detected on a smaller scale, visible only with my binos, a line of marching ants, single file, head to tail, radiating out from their home mound. Having initially focused on the lizard, I wondered about its quest for food, and I thought I would be lucky to see it capture and eat something. Now with my point of view directed at the ants,

I scanned from the mound toward the lizard. I beheld the steady movement of the continuous column of ants, off to a day's work. Then I switched back to the lizard, its body motionless and parked right next to the ant column. I added together my observations so far and realized I was witness to an ambush of innocent marching soldiers. The lizard's tongue fired out, then back in with an ant attached. It turns out horned lizards are known for just exactly this routine-- ambushing ants. In fact most of the ants passed along freely and innocently, apparently unaware that an occasional member of their cadre went missing. They were programmed for the uniform colonial job description of gathering food and caring for their mound. March, march, march. I was impressed with the unstoppable, onward life of the ants, just as I was also impressed with the ambush tactic of the lizard.

Getting outdoors now in New Mexico in search of ants, I was happy to breathe good air and feel the warmth of a pleasant, mild afternoon at 7,000 feet elevation. The air was quiet and windless. The typical noisy birds of earlier morning hours had silenced themselves. I soon spotted an ant mound and stopped just short of the outer margin to become alone with its ants, members of the working caste who were on above-ground duty. I took out my notebook and began. These were the ants I came to see, red harvester ants, genus *Pogonomyrmex*.

I recorded at 2:55 p.m. that the ant mound was in full sunlight. It was a low, circular mound a bit more than six feet in diameter, but shallow and not rising to a height much more than eight inches near the middle. The surface was bare of all plant life and showed a soft texture of tiny red stones, uniform in size, at about an eighth of an inch diameter. These ants worked tediously to maintain the clean surface of their mound. The ants were only about a third of an inch long, which I soon discovered was the reason that I originally felt I saw so few ants, small and red, scattered only here and there around all sides of the mound that was also colored red. Even fewer ants seemed to be coming and going beyond the outer periphery of the mound. The longer I looked, as my eyes adjusted to the bright substrate and the scale of ant body size, the more I realized this was a busy place indeed, with many more ants than I saw originally.

In contrast to bright sunshine on the mound and surrounding open ground, dark rings of shade extended slightly beyond the bases of nearby trees. The open ground held only a few tiny tufts of grass and some small herbs, making for a sparse ground cover. Mats of old, discolored needles beneath the pines and old scales under the junipers produced a cover of slowly decaying mulch that seemed to exclude growth of other plants beneath the trees.

I activated the compass on my phone to establish the north-south-east-west axes of the isolated insect microcosm. I marked the pattern near the mound with a cross of two straight dead twigs I gathered from beneath a nearby pine. I couldn't resist adding a small pinecone to each of the four cardinal twig tips. Now I could project the course of the sun's passage earlier in the day and for the rest of the afternoon, and thus I now understood the mound's optimal exposure to the warming effect of solar radiation, well situated in a large open space. In a larger arena that I estimated to lie within a 10-yard radius of the mound, I counted 14 coniferous trees: 10 pines and just four junipers. These were all small trees, as pines and junipers go, no trunks greater than a foot in diameter. None of the junipers was taller than about 15 feet, and the pines no greater than about 35 feet. This would be designated as a young forest, probably regrown following a fire. Noting that the pine needles were clustered in pairs of just two in each fascicle along the twigs, I confirmed the species as Colorado pinyon pine, *Pinus edulis*, also known as the two-needled pinyon. With its compressed, scaly leaves and ripening, bluish cones, or berries, the common one-seed juniper, *Juniperus monosperma*, was also easy to identify.

As I began to see more and more ants, here and there

over the entire mound, I was able to spot a special area out in the middle, which was a shallow pocket depression of about six inches in diameter. In this little basin I saw two small holes dropping into the ground, each less than half an inch across. A lot of ants were moving in or out, or lingering around these openings. I surveyed all the rest of the mound quickly, a couple of times, and I found no other such place where ants were coming and going. This pocket depression was the portal to what lay below, the secret lives of the ants. I later learned from an ant-ecologist friend about a myth maintained by prospectors in the old west. They believed you should look around ant mounds for little bits of gold. If you found them, you should dig down, for the mother lode.

I squatted down at the edge of the mound and focused my effort now on what single individuals were doing. Most of them were, if carrying anything at all, holding such tiny objects in their mandibles that I could not see them. However a good number of individuals were scurrying along with visible little slivers of grass or other plant parts, certainly seeds among them, which is common for desert harvester ants. However, what caught my special attention were a few ants who had grabbed onto what for them were large medicine balls, namely the cones (technically speaking), or as we more often say berries of nearby junipers. The berries in tow were faintly reddish, probably somewhat aged after falling to the ground, and not as blue and firm as the lovely berries I observed on the trees. These were all about the size of a small pea and in diameter nearly half the length of an ant. The movement of the berries was slow and erratic. To me this appeared rather comical, and then I realized the key element of the comedy: the ant had to move backwards, with the juniper berry in its mandibles, in order to make progress.

During this first observation period in the powerful mid-afternoon heat, the ants were moving along vigorously, pretty speedy I thought. How fast, I wondered? I was not equipped to combine a stopwatch and measuring tape with their movements, but I recalled a classical scientific paper I once collected, from nearly a century ago (1920 to be exact) published in the prestigious *Proceedings of the U.S. National Academy of Sciences.* The scientist, Harlow Shapley, who was intrigued with the speed of ants, recognized that speed depended on temperature—hot ants move fast, cold ants slow. He combined thermometer with stopwatch and meter stick. I checked the results of Shapley's speed trials later. The maximum speed of ants was about two and a half inches per second at around 95 to 100 degrees Fahrenheit; but at 50 degrees speed was reduced to less than 10% of maximum. The fastest speeds translated to about 0.15 miles per hour, which is slow compared to our human walking speed of about three miles per hour. Shapley came up with the amusing perspective that ants could be used as thermometers, by measuring speed in order to predict environmental temperature. He plotted his results on a graph and produced an equation, based on 1,000 speed trials at various temperatures. His equation predicted temperature within one degree of accuracy. Over the past century ant biologists have continued to study all of this and more, taking into account, for example, the reduction in speed due to size of a load the ant is carrying. It was interesting to realize that ant speed was big science 100 years ago, the message being that animal behavior follows the rules of thermal physics. I was just having fun here in Santa Fe watching ants scurrying around about their business, at whatever speed.

Ant biologists apply the term eusociality when they talk about the communal mission and organization of social ants that result from the fact that members of a colony are genetically identical. Although as a biologist I fully recognize this fact, I am often tempted not to think of them merely as automatons or members of a clone. That's because when I look at them, they seem to be individuals. They're each carrying out separate actions, which happen to involve identical kinds of tasks. But in truth the members of a single colony really are all one clone. Wolves, by contrast, form a socially organized, kin-oriented pack that forages together, shares food, and provides vigilance, while not being genetically identical. Rather, the wolves in a pack are only partially related, as parents, offspring, siblings, or through extended kinship. Thus each individual wolf in a pack is genetically distinct and has a distinct personality. The eusociality of ants provides for the remarkable all-for-one behavior of all members of the colony. This is not the stuff of a human society, not by a long shot.

After watching the ants for nearly an hour, I began to feel comfortable recognizing what was routine, normal behavior — another day in the lives of the ants. And that's the point at which I began to find surprises and to detect exceptions to the generality. Just outside the mound, rimming the margin along with other rejecta, I noticed little black cubical chunks of material, neither soil nor rock, and mostly measuring less than half an inch on a side. I picked them up. They were light. I scratched one across my notebook. Charcoal. With no traces of ash and no big pieces of charcoal remaining on the mound, these small, black bits were evidence of a long-ago fire. The absence of charcoal bits from the core of the mound and their presence at the immediate outer margin indicated to me that the ants all had the same response to charcoal, and they had managed to move the charcoal bits off the mound. Order and organization! All part of best practices as recorded in the ant-mound operations manual. This all seemed consistent with the eusocial context. No outliers here. Nobody could decide to keep a pet piece of charcoal out in the middle of the mound. Again, the eusociality theme dictates uniform and consistent behavior, not at all as we have it in our human society. Lacking homogeneity, we humans have to work with our brains to develop social plans that result in at least some degree of cooperation and common goals in our communities and societies.

The charcoal, now remaining only in these tiny

pieces, resulted from a fire in the distant past. Fire is a significant dynamic in our western forests and deserts. It's part of nature. Lightening remains a principal and stunning natural cause of such fires. Human activities, whether intentional or accidental, also promote fires. That amounts to yet another case of human influence on ecosystems, whether small and local or large and regional. Over the past ten thousand years or so, human tribal groups have lived, gathered, hunted, and even cultivated in the arid environment of the American southwest and the northwest of Mexico. The tiny charcoal fragments displaced by ants to the periphery of the mound I observed, could have been derived from a fire associated with an earlier human presence in this place.

My next observation was a new kind of surprise. As I completed my first hour and a half surveying the soft-red surface of uniformly sized, dainty stonelets, arranged so carefully by the ants atop their deeper-underground world, I spotted a tiny speck of sharply contrasting color: a rounded object of deep, bright indigo. I picked it up. About a sixteenth of an inch across, it had a hole in it. A bead. Clear evidence of human presence. I immediately wanted to know from what people it came. I collected the bead in a plastic vial and left my new observation site, but planned to return at the end of the day. More questions were spinning in my mind. I wondered if this bead had perhaps passed through the hands of earlier Tewa-speaking people around the area of modern Santa Fe at some time after the Spaniards established themselves here nearly 500 years ago.

Just before 8 p.m. the sun scattered deep soft orange against pinyons and junipers on eastern hills as it dropped to the western horizon. The ground in my piece of woodland was no longer illuminated with solar radiation. Only a few ants, moving slowly, remained on the surface, concentrated around the pocket depression containing the holes leading below. The pocket's shape and location had changed, perhaps as much as a foot away from where I originally saw it. Hundreds of ant-hours had been expended on the mound during my short absence of three hours. The insects had moved the little red stonelets around to reconfigure the entrance, gradually, gradually, and it now appeared they were filling in the pocket depression, preparing to close the holes, seemingly part of their routine for concluding the day's activities. To me, these gradual shifts in position of stonelets and the entry pocket leading into underground tunnels were all just random drift in the general architectural plan. The mound was dynamic, but it fulfilled the genetic program for this species. Down below lay the vast cavernous network of food lockers and brood chambers.

As I stared and wondered, another surprise jumped out. A couple of feet away from the new depression containing the portals to the underground rested yet another eye-catching indigo bead, identical to the first. I picked it up in awe and added it to my container. A few days later, on an inspection following an afternoon thundershower that had fully suspended all ant activity, I found yet another bead. The third bead was greenish-turquoise, and a bit larger than the first two beads.

In my quest to meet ants alone, in solitude, in nature, I was surprised to encounter evidence of previous human presence. Perhaps a fire, with its charcoal remains removed by the ants to the mound's periphery. But the beads, similar in size to the red gravel bits and clearly a sign of human presence, were allowed by the ants to remain right in among the millions of tiny stonelets of the same size on the mound. When I later showed the beads to my museum's Native American ethnology specialists, they indicated that these were glass beads of European origin, probably from what is now the Czech Republic. Thus their age could be no greater than the beginning of Spanish settlement and trade in that empire's nearly 500-year-old past. As one of my colleagues finally pointed out, the brightness of the beads suggests they were newer, and unlikely to be from the earliest time of bead trade between the indigenous people and the Spaniards.

Humans and ants have different places and perspectives in nature. The beads I found were imported, traded, and crafted by humans into a decoration. That decoration deteriorated, and its pieces returned to Earth's local ecosystem, where the beads became just three more common stonelets for ants to arrange on their mound. Nothing special for the ants, who simply tarried and performed their duties, transporting and arranging the materials that made up their mound. Beyond such basic site maintenance, the ants' hunting, gathering, and marching assured the flow of nutrition into the lower chambers where reproductive and incubating operations sustained colony life. The beads were ignored by the ants for what we would have valued. The charcoal bits were ejected, without cause for the ants to identify or appreciate them.

I invited myself into the pinyon-juniper woodland and found its ants. I connected with the ant perspective. Their business was serious. It was survival. They allowed me to bend down and peer into the midst of their society. I was curious about them, but they were not curious about me and my human views.

It is our privilege to take time to get out and explore places where we can see into nature. Nature still works, and always will, in so many ways that are independent of humans and our domineering transformation of Earth. It's good to put ourselves out into pure nature, just for the pleasure of sensing how she works. As a biologist who knows many other animals better than ants, I loved the simplicity of this brief acquaintance with ants. I came without the bias of a scientific agenda. I saw the world through other eyes and appreciated this modest sample of the beauty of nature.

3

TAKING A WALK
WITH A BEAVER

I never before thought of taking a walk with a beaver, but on a fine New England evening in the final days of spring the opportunity arose. I was charmed by the quiet but majestic rural campus of one of the region's many historic small colleges, where I visited for a week on retreat with friends. Stately brick buildings and neatly mowed lawns made up the campus layout. At the front of the school, on the main street of town, a signpost adorned with numerous pointing arrows set the global context of the small town. One of the arrows, directed toward London, England, indicated 5,386 kilometers.

The beauty I saw in the campus arose from the natural terrain and the arboretum-like array of trees, many old giants, tall and broad-crowned fellows of many varieties, both natives of eastern North America and visitors from other continents. Water also distinguished this place—a gentle stream that edged along the bottom of a slope that descended down from the main street up at the crest of the hill. The shaded waterway flowed slowly now in late spring and widened into an even more captivating space: Lower Lake. Although an artificial dam now helped to retain water in Lower Lake, I imagined an earlier time when dams here were constructed by the primordial and proper engineers of this ecosystem, the beavers.

Beavers are rodents. They are behemoths compared to their tiny mouse cousins. As the largest rodent species in North America, beavers can reach 50, 60 even 70 pounds. They employ their enormous, thick, broad front teeth (incisors) to cut down large trees and snip off edible smaller branches and leaves. Succulent alders, willows, and aspens top the list of beaver favorites. Just two incisors above and two below, the big up-front teeth are followed in the jaw by a long gap without any teeth at all. Finally toward the rear emerge the low, flat-topped premolars and molars, four in number, above and below, left and right. It's their job to grind the ingested plant materials before the beaver can swallow them. When working in the tree-felling and pruning mode, the beaver projects its lower jaw forward so the upper and lower incisors meet to do their cutting job, while the edges of the lips simply close over the palate and across the toothless gap. Thus the big, busy, buck-teeth actually remain outside the closed-off mouth. (We humans can't do that!) No dirt and wood chips to get into your mouth, Beaver, while tree-chopping. For chewing and grinding, the beaver shifts its lower jaw backwards so the rear set of teeth engage, above and below.

The beaver denizens of our North American waterways live, by preference and practice, a modest and simplified vegetarian existence: leaves, tender twigs, and bark for their fare. It just happens they perform the remarkable feat of bringing down entire trees. This adds up to a physical impact on the environment of a major scale, namely the formation of dams that hold back streams into ponds or small lakes and lead, in turn, over time, to redevelopment of landscape into new meadows and riparian woodlands. Ecologists consider the beaver an ecosystem engineer. Formerly holding its influence over most of the United States, the beaver has been largely extirpated from the land that humans took over for their exclusive use. But the beaver abounds across more northerly reaches of North America, over the grand, expansive salad bowl of aspen and willow that covers much of Canada and Alaska. This is all prime real estate and *prima cucina*, if you're a beaver.

Small, liberal arts colleges in the United States engender exploration of all that life offers in a nurturing, protective environment. This college provided protection not only to its students but also to its large succulent trees surrounding Lower Lake. Hefty and handsome trunks of oak and birch, and smaller flowering cherries near water's edge were encased in cylinders of heavy wire grid. Anti-beaver defense.

This sort of measure—restraining beavers from pursuit of their natural inclination to fell trees, to consume tender twigs and leaves, and to engineer an ecosystem—is typical of the disposition that our own human species exercises over other species. Some people believe we should take all opportunities to hold dominion over Earth and her creatures and their habitats. Sometimes this human domination of nature is considered to be management, sometimes it is just exploitation, and sometimes dominion and control are involved in conservation strategy.

Most recently we have recognized the enormous impact of our massive human population on the balance of what remains on our planet. We have in some instances preserved habitats and their species by excluding or limiting our own presence. But in many other cases we continue to exploit natural spaces and their living inhabitants in order to meet our human demands for use of space on our own terms. In the present case of beavers and trees on a college campus, the seemingly reasonable choice was to preserve some trees. Sometimes it's hard to imagine the management approach that humans will take. Who needs to win? Who loses? We like trees. We like beavers, or at least I do.

I did not have access to the college's written policy of landscape management. But I did see examples of their decisions, starting with the anti-beaver cages around the trees. I sympathized with how that choice was made, as it has been made in many other places.

Regarding another campus policy, I read signs posted around Lower Lake that expressed the college's view of Canada geese. These waterfowl were absent during my visit in late spring, but apparently they frequented, or attempted to frequent, the shores of Lower Lake at other times. Or were geese gone because they read the goose-unfriendly signs?

"Please don't feed the geese! They graze on grass and don't need it." I easily imagined the basis of this decision—to protect the lake's shores from deposits of goose poop. This, in turn, protected the soles (of the shoes) of students, if not their souls. I questioned the sign's wording: "don't need it." Did they mean grass? Grass is good food for a grazer. A grazer is one who eats grass, by grazing. Geese need food. That's just basic biology. My further analysis of the sign revealed other aspects of attitude and culture. I wondered whether members of the English Department would find "graze on grass" to be redundant. And the Music Department certainly has promoted J. S. Bach's familiar pastoral aria (ninth movement of cantata BWV No. 208) that bears the touching title *Schafe Können Sicher Weiden,* recognized by those who don't read German as *Sheep May*

Safely Graze. But students here, whether majoring in music or biology, might wonder, "Why not geese too?"

The goose sign continued: "Feeding them makes them aggressive toward people. It can hurt the geese as well, increasing crowding and leading to disease such as avian cholera, avian botulism, and duck plague." This frightening discourse appeared to present the case for geese as unwelcome carriers of deadly diseases. And then maybe crowded populations of geese would overtake the world? It might have been more parsimonious simply to say: "We don't want geese hanging out here and pooping, so please don't feed them." You never know what you'll get when you set up a college committee to address a problem.

Our bigger human question of controlling other species is complex and related to the perceived value of any particular species under consideration. Our decisions typically favor human needs and whims over the needs of other species. Or they favor, perhaps arbitrarily, the presence of one animal or plant species over another, or the presence of prey species over their predators, or a charismatic species over a plain and perhaps not-so-charismatic species. The goals of the college appeared to be protection of students and lawns, not geese, and protection of trees, while discouraging beavers. Of course these are the same decisions that have been made in favor of people, lawns, and trees in many other human-occupied landscapes and waterscapes where we and our managed spaces are inconvenienced by the presence of wildlife.

My first day on campus I tried to imagine the pristine setting that prevailed when earlier, indigenous people lived, hunted, and gathered around this place—the forest and the stream. I also wondered about the first European settlers and later the founders of the college and how they changed the landscape first with farming and forestry practices, and later with horticulture and landscaping. The original deciduous forest held maple, oak, and alder. Associated evergreens included fir, pine, and hemlock. I wondered what numbers of beavers originally thrived along the waterway and fed on the natural riparian vegetation. Clearly, in the meantime, the college's plan was not fully compatible with the practices of beaver life.

The campus placed great value on its trees, many of which were historic biological icons that stood tall among academic buildings. An enormous North American native red oak, with a trunk diameter that I stepped off at about eight feet, towered above a four-story building. A metal placard named it as *Quercus rubra* E00356-6. A copper beech, *Fagus sylvatia* E00374-1, native to Europe, with an eight-foot trunk diameter, supported a crown of some 120 feet in diameter that enshrouded the library. These old and magnificent giants are specimens of incredible beauty and enduring value.

I had seen from the early moments of my arrival certain encouraging signs of beaver along the waterways: telltale tooth marks on loose branches at the water's edge, a few small cut-off stumps. I wondered how many beavers lived here now. And how did they get along with the college?

Lower Lake spread out just below where I often sat writing at my desk, peering out from my second-story window at the glassy surface and serenity of this quiet body of water. My abode was a simple college dormitory room, but the view was exquisite. Down below, near the shore, a lone Adirondack chair invited any passer-by to sit at the edge of Lower Lake and watch the open water, the surrounding shores, and the vegetation at the land-water interface. From my vantage point I enjoyed fixing on the lake and imagining what was going on inside — down on the muddy bottom, in the cool, mid waters, at the warm surface, and all around the perimeter, a bank crowded with reeds, bushes, and small alder and willow trees. The college proudly reports on a lakeside sign that the American eel still moves upstream into Lower Lake on its migratory quest for survival. These young fish return all the way from the Sargasso Sea, out in the mid Atlantic Ocean, to this protected New England sanctuary. As I stared out, people occasionally passed quietly on the pathway below, with other thoughts and impressions of the lake on their minds.

Shoreward from the path, the grassy surface reached downward through scattered birch, maple, alder, and willows, down to fresh mud. The lake mud smelled alive when I stepped down there in mid-morning sun. Bullfrogs issued deep galumphs from their nearby stations. Chipmunks ventured out from a haven of low juniper shrubs to scurry across open spaces.

My thoughts returned to beavers and their history alongside humans. I once collected an old pamphlet issued by the United States Department of Agriculture, dated October 18, 1922, to be exact. Authored by Vernon Bailey (1864-1942), Chief Field Naturalist at the Bureau of Biological Survey, the twenty-nine-page text of Bulletin No. 1078 began with the following paragraph.

"Only two centuries ago beavers inhabited the greater part of the North American continent and were to the native people an important source of food and warm clothing. Their fur soon attracted the white traders and trappers, and traffic in their skins became an important factor in promoting the early settlement of the country. Through the generations of intensive trapping that followed, the beavers were greatly reduced in numbers and restricted in range until they have been exterminated over much of their area. For the last 20 years they have been given special protection in many sections of the country and after being long absent have been restored to some parts of their old range, where under favorable conditions they have thrived and increased rapidly."

I was pleased to be reminded of the importance of beavers in the lives of Native Americans and also of the subsequent historic role of beavers in the white settlement of North America. Bulletin 1078 further informed readers of beaver-human conflict in the form of damage to agriculture and other human activities. It suggested means of controlling beavers, including moving them to wild areas where they might be better "conserved as a valuable and interesting natural resource." The possibility of commercial beaver farming was also promoted by the pamphlet. The USDA has always been about helping Americans to find economic success based on our natural resources. On a culinary note, Chief Bailey pointed out that beaver liver and tail were "especial delicacies" and furthermore that the body meat "was generally preferred by trappers to any other game, even in the early days when buffalo, elk, and deer were abundant." A nice pot of rodent stew, anyone? The pamphlet was, as indicated on the last page, originally available for free distribution by the Department, but additional pamphlets were available for fifteen cents per copy.

Surely our feelings toward the beaver have changed, even as most contemporary human inhabitants of North America have never even seen one, let alone spent serious time with a free-living beaver. Our human species, dominator of our transformed Earth, has greatly reduced the beaver's natural geographic range and abundance. We have disregarded its role as an ecosystem engineer. Beavers are the ones who originally managed many of our North American waterways and associated lands, working tirelessly to conserve soil and water as they preserved landscapes. We miss them now for the formerly much greater extent of their influence. But the beaver is still here, in its own way. Anyone with the desire can know a beaver, with some effort and patience. I have had the pleasure of watching them on many occasions, but during my busy week on this campus it would require an element of serendipity for my path to cross that of a beaver.

It was seeming that my opportunity to see a beaver during this week in New England was going to remain an unrealized dream, especially after several more days of not seeing a beaver. My musings about the college's unwelcome measures against beavers and geese had left me suspicious that I had no chance to see a beaver, much less take a walk with one. But it happened.

In the cool of evening twilight and with other thoughts in mind, I headed out by myself for an after-dinner stroll. I crossed a footbridge at the lower end of the lake and reached a pathway that directed me along the far side of the lake. The sky above showed a clear and deepening, darkening blue. Among the subdued tones down below on the flat lake surface, as I peered through tree trunks along the shoreline, I spotted something — a subtle form, quiet, mostly submerged and with a relaxed posture and very slow movement. I stopped behind a tree so as not to be seen and in hopes that it would continue to behave naturally. I wanted to be sure about the size of the animal; it needed to be big enough to be a beaver rather than a smaller muskrat. Now I was sure. It was an average sized beaver, not too big. I was afraid he would become aware of my movement, slap his tail on the water, dive down, and disappear, to end a typical brief but enjoyable beaver sighting. What he did, however, continued to surprise me over the course of about fifteen minutes that we would end up spending together.

I realized later, as I began to relish what was happening, that I had no reason for designating this beaver in my mind as a male. As a biologist, I would normally want to know whether an individual is female or male. Knowing an animal's gender could account for some of the behaviors I might observe. However, I did not know the animal's sex, and perhaps I thought of the beaver as "he" just because I had connected with this swimming rodent and wanted to personify him. Now he simply continued to swim slowly along the shoreline, which was paralleled by the trail on which I continued to walk.

His pace over the lake's surface seemed to remain constant, and I decided to get into lock-step to match his speed—very slow, his stroke by stroke with my step by step. We were synchronized. Only his head and upper back, at most, protruded above the surface. No aspect of his four limbs rose near enough to the surface to cause an additional ripple. Although I wanted him to lift the famously broad and flat scaly tail enough to provide a view, I could not see evidence of the tail. The sky was providing less and less light. I raised my brow muscles and attempted to widen my view, opening my eyes as big as I could. Despite my anticipations of what he would or would not do, I remained deeply moved with the prolonged connection I was experiencing with this animal I had so greatly hoped to see. This was, after all, the creature that I felt really belonged here in the lake. As we continued together, he seemed to be doing nothing in particular. He was out on a stroll in early evening at just the time I had chosen to do the same.

The beaver swam a bit closer to shore, perhaps now just ten yards out, and just below me. This was the closest we'd gotten to one another. He stopped. I stopped. I sensed that he was aware of my presence, and I again suspected that our encounter was about to end. But it did not. He waited. I waited. I peered down into the water, clear but dark, and hard for me to see detail. Yet enough skylight still remained that I could now see just an inch or so below the surface and behind the beaver a reflection of that light against a broad oval form being elevated. Wondrous, the tail of the beaver! It remained below the surface.

He resumed his forward movement. I resumed,

matching beaver tempo, a slow, relaxed, twilight mode. The suspense continued to mount, simply from his doing nothing more than just cruising slowly, neither diving nor disappearing. He clearly was going nowhere in a hurry. No other beavers were to be seen on the lake. By random happenstance, no other people came walking along the trail. We continued, my steps matching the gentle strokes and propulsion of his legs and tail, coupled only with his subtle steering, none of which I was actually able to see below the surface. We reached the upstream end of the lake. I didn't want this to end.

As I approached a point where my view down to the lake surface would become obscured, I stopped, only because continuing would have ended my relationship with Beaver. He had reached the end of the lake, but he did not stop. Instead he circled outward in a small loop and then came right back. He circled again, and then a third time. This was more curious. What was he doing? Finally he paused and dove, forward and down. He disappointed me by not revealing his tail above water. Now I could only wait and watch. Was he gone?

Within less than a minute he returned to the surface and surprised me with a piece of cargo in his mouth, something long and dark—a muddy, old branch that had no doubt been on the bottom for a long time. This was not a fresh dinner morsel. He manipulated the old branch playfully in his mouth a couple of times and let it drop. This was not foraging behavior. This was most likely what behaviorists would call "displacement activity," something you do just to occupy time and when you might be concerned with something else, like a man on shore who's watching you and making you feel self-conscious.

It was time to say good-bye. I have watched beavers before, swimming strongly in rivers, moving branches around their damming operations, escaping human attention with a warning tail slap on the water followed by a disappearing dive. This beaver did none of those things. He and I were at ease, out for a stroll. We connected. I was delighted. I cared more about him because he appeared to be paying attention to me — an experience of mutual awareness.

Slowly he turned toward the center of the lake and swam outward, in no hurry. He dropped gently beneath the dark, smooth plane of water, disappearing from my sight and leaving only a tiny ripple on the surface of Lower Lake.

4

LONE EGRET IN A LAGOON

The big Río Ameca flows into Banderas Bay at the border of the Mexican states of Nayarit and Jalisco, carrying the last of its valued waters to reach the Pacific Ocean from high-above canyons in the Sierra de la Primavera. Its flow varies from minimal in the dry season to moderate in the wet season. Beyond that, the river swells occasionally to a torrent that rages downward from the sierra. Such a remarkable event stands out as a rare year, when the river's powerful and damaging erosive forces reshape the landscape by changing the course of the waterways and relocating rocks and soils. Where the Ameca's fresh water joins the sea's salt water, the contents of two ecosystems mix together to benefit the interface. Organic nutrients and minerals from the continent support the ocean's beneficiaries: algae, plankton, larval creatures, fish, and birds, to name a few.

A few miles south of the Ameca's entry into the sea and at a much smaller scale, an isolated stream, not currently captured by its big brother the Ameca, flows modestly into the bay on its own. The fact that this little river does not belong to the big network of the Ameca basin is just a random result of geological ups and downs in the recent shape of Earth's surface.

I found this little stream, the Río Pitillal, one warm and sunny winter morning as I walked along the beach. Breaking waves and the high tide of the previous night had delivered a large lens of sand to the head of the beach, which closed the stream's mouth and held back a tiny lagoon.

Local children, who belonged to families out to enjoy a Sunday outing on the beach, waded in and out of the lagoon. Other children played on the ocean side of the sand bar in the saltwater wash that pulsed up the beach from gently rolling waves that were breaking along the shoreline. A few other kids played right at the crest of the sand bar, where a little trickle, just a few inches wide, flowed toward the sea, and these industrious kids, looking very pleased with themselves, were bulldozing sand with their hands to dam off the seaward flow of water that was trying to escape from the lagoon. Finally, a few other kids, just next to the dam-building crew, were starting a side channel to divert the lagoon's water around the dam.

I walked easily across the soft wet sand of the berm and passed to the north bank of the Pitillal, which was reinforced just upstream by large rocks that created a steep bank. This supported a headland that held a grove of tall coconut palms with fronds that moved gently in the morning breeze. I turned back immediately to pursue my curiosity for the lagoon. As I re-crossed the stream, I found myself among the playing children, as other adults brushed by on their morning walks.

Also moving right in among us, just five or six feet

from me, was a lone white wading bird, a bit taller than a foot in height, attentively walking with its gaze fixed in the shallow water around its long black legs. Through the clear water I noticed the bird's brilliant yellow feet stepping smartly along in water only a few inches deep at the edge of the lagoon. This was a snowy egret, with the Mexican name garza dedos dorados, referring to its golden toes, which contrasted sharply with the jet black legs. To ornithologists this is *Egretta thula*, a member of the heron family, Ardeidae. Among various egret species, it's pretty much medium sized, at just less than a pound, and with a wing span of about three feet.

It seemed to me a special pleasure to encounter just this one, solitary egret in this place and in this moment — in the mouth of a little river and in a small pool of estuarine water that was just now being temporarily held back by beach sands, before it would ultimately enter the sea. I felt a simplicity here at the terminus of this small river that originated only in the nearby hills and amounted to such a minor source alongside the much bigger regional waterway of the Ameca. I was out and about quietly on my own, and the egret was on its own. And this was where we met.

The egret worked alone, in the absence of fellow competitors of her own kind. She impressed me somehow, as I stood at the mouth of the river and looked upstream into the lagoon. Why was she alone? I had earlier watched five of these same egrets together, just a short distance south of the stream, where they stood on the big rocks of a jetty and made short feeding forays together, flying down into the sand at the upper reaches of the noisy surf rolling up the beach.

The lone egret I was watching in the Pitillal lagoon impressed me with her foraging style and success, and with her gentle demeanor. I remained at the side to watch her for another half hour. She repeatedly struck her long and slender black beak into the water, often penetrating the sand slightly — this was innate, routine feeding behavior. I noticed also the yellow coloring around the base of her bill, a complement to the yellowness of her feet. She picked off and swallowed successive captures of small micro-crustaceans (shrimp, crabs, and such) and likely other food items, most of which I could not actually see at the interface of water and sand around the base of her legs. I wondered if she could feel the moving prey with the sensitivity of her feet. Did the color of her feet actually attract prey? She appeared to detect moving prey visually, with the penetrating focus of her yellow eyes, as the prey moved above the sand near her feet. She stood upright to swallow, making an obvious ripple down her throat. When a small breeze caught her neck and head just right, the telltale lengthy silky plumes on top and at the nape of her neck extended out momentarily, adding a decorative touch of elegance to her appearance.

Then I realized one more thing, remarkable, yet obvious, that allowed her to work so steadily and successfully, and that was her seeming disregard for me and the boisterous play of children. Ignoring humans — most all gentle souls, typically minding their own business — had to be something she had learned after dismissing her basic egret instincts to flee from large awkward primates. Certainly she had her peripheral vision turned on, just in case. But her effective focus was on obtaining food. Good food, readily available where the little stream met the sea. And she was the only egret taking advantage of this opportunity on the morning I met her.

I don't really know whether this lone egret's foraging performance was above average or below for her species. Nor do I know whether my arbitrary female gender assignment was correct. The sexes are very similar in size and appearance. I was confident to know that she belonged to a successful gene pool of a single species that stretches over an enormous geographic range from Canada to Patagonia. I was delighted by my encounter with this bird in the solitude and serenity that we both found in a small Mexican lagoon.

In its last stretches approaching the sea at Banderas Bay, the Río Pitillal becomes a modified and controlled channel. It flows through the greater urban area of Puerto Vallarta, populated by a quarter of a million people. I hope, in my own optimism, that the citizens here will persist in their protection of the precious Río Pitillal, as it continues to pass through their land and link them to the sea. We all share in the concern for care and protection, as we continue to settle everywhere on our planet.

I also trust that others may continue to find the kind of joy that I was able to experience out in nature on this ordinary day. It was just by chance that the flow of a Mexican lagoon happened to pause so that a lone egret and I could meet at the same place and time.

5

SMELT MATING ON A BEACH

PREDATOR BONANZA

Evening twilight in Washington's San Juan Islands archipelago brings serenity to the day's end, a quietness that settles in before dark. The length of midsummer evenings prolongs the opportunity to experience the wonders of this place where the sea meets with beaches and bluffs lined with coniferous forest. The smells of fir and pine mix in the warm early evening air with odors of salt water and biologically active mud and sand where the tides move up and down the beaches twice a day.

For more than a decade in my early retirement I came to know and enjoy the varied landscapes and seascapes that comprise this natural wonderland—each bay, each beach, each forest grove of Douglas fir, western hemlock, grand fir, red cedar, shore pine, Sitka spruce, madrona, and the deciduous alder and maple. These places provided new experiences, whether on pleasant walking trails or on the water, by kayak or canoe, by boat, or on one of the big ferries that wind their routes through the islands. My base was a cabin along a low bluff, above a narrow sandy beach at the top of gently sloping muddy tidelands in a shallow and productive bay. A dock provided the connection between the surrounding marine waters and the cabin in the uplands.

On many evenings I stepped down the stairs to the dock after sunset to smell the cooling air and peer outward across the water's surface, quieted by the absence of breezes that had stirred the air and driven waves across the bay during the bright and sunny afternoon. In early twilight, crows flew by or clambered around in tree branches above the shore. An occasional raven passed on noisy wings flapping in the still air, perhaps sounding off with its signature deep "honk" that resonated more distinctively in twilight than during the busier soundscape of the day. Bald eagles passed by now and then, continuing on alert for the last foraging opportunities before nightfall. River otters cruised slowly across the bay, often as many as four or five in a group, occasionally raising their tapered tails in an arc as they slipped below for a short dive. Harbor seals, usually just single individuals, floated quietly, barely moving, as if in twilight repose, occasionally lifting their big heads above the water.

This evening was another such visit to the dock. I carried with me a bucket containing Dungeness crab body parts from a festive harvest we had made earlier in the day that resulted in our dinner fare. It was customary to recycle the inedible remainders of the crabs back into the ecosystem, giving the satisfaction that natural decomposition would contribute to ongoing life in the bay — the next generations of crabs and other creatures in the food chain. Scattering my bucket's contents across the quiet water out at the end of the dock produced a noisy splash.

Returning toward the shore, I gazed back at the bank, hoping perhaps to spot a mink or a raccoon, the semiaquatic mammals who often moved along foraging among boulders and logs at the bottom of the bluff. I noticed from the position of the waterline along the shore that the tide was approaching a high mark and covering most of the upper strip of sandy beach. A small remaining band of exposed sand at the base of the bluff was fine and gray, but mixed with small gravel and larger white chips of clam shells that had eroded out of the top of the bluff. These clam-shell fragments, dated by archaeologists as 800 years old, came from middens deposited by indigenous people who earlier harvested here and nourished themselves with the abundance of the bay.

With all the common seashore wildlife on my mind, I was unprepared for what next unfolded before my eyes — the mating ritual of smelt, an event that always took me by surprise. You have to be in the right place at just the right moment to see these remarkable little fish in the act. But this was such an evening. As I walked back along the dock toward shore, I became a voyeur of thousands of swarming smelt, whose females moved ashore at high tide to deposit eggs in the highest sands at the head of the beach, even as the males showed up to shed clouds of their spermy solution over the eggs being released by the females.

Fluttering and splashing sounds first alerted me to a spot back on the shoreline. Goose bumps popped on my arms and body as I ran excitedly shoreward to the base of the dock. I saw flashing silver fish bodies tumbling over one another in the sand at the water's edge, wiggling back and forth in sideways arcs to excavate shallow depressions in which the females placed their eggs. Probably several hundred smelt all together were making this single localized commotion in a space of only a few feet along the shoreline, mostly in water only a few inches deep. In all the frenzy a few bodies were cast completely out of the water onto bare sand. The previously clear water was clouded from the turbulence of sand stirred up by the moving fish and from another source: the milky whiteness from the huge volume of sperm being released by the males.

From my previous experience here I knew that I could move back out along the dock to the deeper water behind me to see huge schools of fish from which the spawners were peeling off toward the shore. Staring down through three or four feet of clear water at the sharp image of cobbles dotting the mud bottom, suddenly I saw a swiftly moving dark cloud that eclipsed the bay's bottom, as thousands of tightly clustered smelt swam rapidly under the dock, parallel to the shore, perhaps taking ten seconds or so until they were all gone. Moments later another school passed by. Then again another black cloud in the water below, with occasional tiny instantaneous silver flashes from single members of the school who must have turned sideways momentarily, making them stand out visually from the safety-in-numbers of the otherwise uniformly dark-colored school as viewed from above.

These common forage fish, about six inches long, are formally known as surf smelt, *Hypomesus pretiosus*, members of the smelt family, Osmeridae. They are covered with smooth scales and delicate skin, bright silvery on the sides, but with a dark stripe along the mid side and darker color on top as well. Populations of this species can be found from southern California to Alaska. Smelt are especially successful in the San Juan Islands, where they mate in every month of the year. Like other forage fish, they occupy the middle of the food chain, as consumers of small plankton and as objects of predation by larger fish, and even whales. Having sex where the surf meets the upper reaches of beach sand is not unique to the smelt family, as members of two other fish families also practice this behavior: the sand lances (Ammodytidae) and silver sides (Atherinidae). I first witnessed spawning in sand at high tide by grunion (of the silver side family) along a southern California beach as a graduate student on an ichthyology class field trip.

The original mating cluster of smelt in the sand near the dock had dispersed, but they amounted to only a small fraction of all the masses of fish I could now see swimming back and forth in deeper water along the shore. As I looked further up the beach, beyond hearing distance, I spotted a different commotion. A harbor seal I'd seen earlier had beached itself at the shoreline and was floundering about in water that was unusually shallow for a seal seeking a meal. I was surprised to see this big mammal biting at the water line, snapping up the mating smelt. And now, closer to me, an otter swam up to the shoreline to indulge in the feast, another predator to exploit the mating frenzy. Once the fish arrived at the upper reaches of fine gravel and sand and began their reflexive egg depositions and sperm ejaculations, they were mindless of anything other than their sexual performance. Unfortunately, that meant they were being eaten alive by predators at the very moment they were successfully accomplishing life's ultimate act of producing the next generation. Sad and ironic, it seemed. But this was real biology, nature. I observed that the otter and the seal both fed directly with their mouths, the seal grabbing more with each bite than the otter. The seal secured the fish inside its big mouth (no hands available on this flippered mammal), and then, with little in the way of chewing, it gulped them down. The otter, in contrast, used its paws to secure the fish into its mouth as it bit down to kill and break up the fish a bit before swallowing.

After soaking up the initial excitement of the mating ritual, I began to realize that the spawning event was turning into a bonanza for alert predators. And upon that thought, my next was to become a predator myself. I had often previously spent a few minutes scooping up smelt when I happened upon spawning down at the dock. I ran to the cabin for a bucket and net, and I called for my daughter to come along. "Smelt!" I yelled, which was enough to elicit her immediate participation. We dashed down a pathway to the beach and found ourselves among fish who were unaware of us. Leaning down and scooping with the net, and even with the bucket itself, it was only a matter of a few seconds of sweeping at the fluttering, splashing turmoil before we obtained several dozen of these marvelous creatures. Enough. They would make for a fine fish fry for breakfast the next morning, and the rest could be used as bait.

If the thrill of witnessing the mating smelt, observing a seal and an otter exploiting the masses of fish, and finally catching a few of them wasn't enough, yet another predatory player showed up for the grand finale. Looking up from our bucket and net operation, we saw a bald eagle dropping down to land at the water line in a mass of fish. The eagle stood among the smelt, barely talons-deep and only about twenty-five feet away from us. The giant bird picked off the fish one at a time with its massive beak, manipulating and crushing them briefly, then flexing its neck as it swallowed. The bird continued this for several minutes, and we didn't count how many it ate. Probably due to our mutual proximity, the eagle cast seemingly nervous glances at us as it ate voraciously. Sharing this further moment of predation by the great avian symbol of the USA provided a final cap to a splendid outdoor evening.

The pressure of all the predation I was privileged to observe on smelt in the early twilight of this summer evening made me question the timing of the fishes' mating. Wouldn't they be less likely to be exploited by visually capable predators if they waited a while for the more clandestine cover of a darker sky? Apparently the fish biologists working in the area have not fully assessed the times of day and night when the smelt mate in different months of the year. The timing is already known to be complex because the fish have to seek out the hours when tides are relatively high in order to deposit fertilized eggs in the sands higher up along the beaches. Nature's actions and reactions are indeed complex and met with the need for compromise and trade-offs. My experience, in this case, amounted to seeing the balance tipped in favor of several species of predators, who placed a small dent in the smelt population. Witnessing the reality of multiple predators exploiting a prey population changed my sense of the balance of nature in this system.

On a separate amusing occasion, a few years later, I observed, again by chance, spawning smelt in evening twilight. This time the fish were met by just a single predator who happened by on the spur of the moment. This was a mink, that slender, glistening-brown, furry mammal, only about a foot and a half long, much smaller than the otter. Once this agile fellow spotted the smelt ritual, he became about as oblivious to me as the smelt were to him. Standing at water's edge, he simply plunged his face into the noisy swarm and immediately emerged with a single smelt in his mouth. He applied a kill-bite, manipulated the fish briefly with his paws, turned back toward the bluff, and trundled off to cache his booty out of sight behind a huge bolder. He repeated this six more times, accumulating a very significant stash. This caching behavior allowed him to harvest more fish in total than if he'd stopped to chew up and swallow pieces of each fish. As the smelt had mostly subsided into slightly deeper water, the mink stepped up for a curtain call, showing off yet another good piece of mink behavior. Sliding forward and disappearing below the surface in a dive that lasted only about five seconds, he then popped back out of the water with a flipping silver prize in his gape. He paused briefly to apply the kill-bite and ran off to add this encore piece to his cache for a total of eight smelt—a major haul for this alert little predator.

Although I have often seen smelt spawning on the beach, the observation of several different kinds of predators converging on a single evening's spawning event within a matter of minutes remains one of my most memorable nature experiences in the islands. Of course my own personal observations are hardly unique to the full range of nature's regular happenings. This particular memory was just personal, to me, and resulted simply because I happened to show up at a time when nature's serendipity allowed me to witness her actions. I love to call that a special *moment in nature*. To seek patiently that special moment, we just have to go outdoors and pay attention.

6

GECKO AMBUSH

You would hardly think the porch light at the door of a little beach apartment where I stayed in Mexico was a place to observe nature. But my nighttime experience with the building's resident reptiles, some dainty geckos, gave me a new view of nature and a fond memory. The small lizards I watched there had adjusted their natural foraging behavior to take advantage of tiny flying and crawling insects that were attracted by the light and heat coming from behind the shields covering the light bulbs outside each door in the building. The shield, a specially molded tile about a foot in height, was plastered on two sides into the stucco wall and open at the top and bottom. This arrangement formed an excellent food-attracting chamber and nighttime ambush hideout for a gecko. The lizards simply waited in anticipation, clinging easily to the vertical wall surface by the touch of their special toe pads that also helped them to dart over and grab any unsuspecting dinner item that entered the trap. Easy come, easy go.

It became a pleasant routine for me, each time I ventured out or returned at night, to check the light in front of my door. I also explored around the other doors in the passageway leading up the stairs to my room. This was especially fun after my own evening out dining at one of the restaurants in town. The gecko check served as my final, end-of-the-day nature ritual—how were the geckos dining this evening?

As I approached a porch light, the lizard was sometimes fully visible, though more usually only part was sticking out the top or bottom of the cover—the huge head or the tip of the thin tail at the end of the gecko's roughly four-inch-long body. Other times the lizard was completely hidden to my view until I looked up from beneath to discover the ambusher in waiting, motionlessly fixed against the wall that was painted in a light, earthy tone.

On more playful occasions I performed my lizard check differently. If I saw no lizard just above or below the shield, I would walk up to the light and slap the wall beneath the fixture with my hand. Any would-be ambusher inside would then pop out the top like a jack-in-the box, alarmed by my momentary disruption of lizard business. If I pursued further, the gecko might scurry upward toward the ceiling, quickly out of my eager reach. Once in a while I managed to land the palm of my hand and fingers gently atop one of these creatures against the wall, and then nestle it into my hand, and finally to fix it between the fingers of one hand for a minute of visual inspection and touching with the fingers of the other hand. My left-hand hold on the gecko consisted of the thumb and forefinger grasping the gecko's shoulder and the fourth and fifth fingers holding the hips and tail base. Thus immobilized by my careful hold, the lizard was available for study of its external anatomy.

The big head on the small body of the geckos seemed to be an exaggeration. The eyes were huge and had vertically oriented, black, slit-like pupils, not round like ours. Looking these lizards in the eye you could see no eyelid. Instead they had a transparent membrane for protection. The general body color was light tan, a bit blotchy, and also somewhat pinkish or yellowish, with soft and thin skin that appeared to be semitransparent. You thought you were looking right through to internal organs. A tiny hole behind the mouth was the ear opening. The toes were remarkable for their elaborate pads, with little microstructures that somehow help the gecko to stick to and climb on vertical surfaces. The scales covering the body were relatively uniform, except for some larger ones along the back. All of this, together with our locality, was sufficient to suggest that this was the common house gecko *Hemidactylus frenatus*.

On one occasion when I slapped the stucco beneath a light shield, the fleeing lizard was seemingly so startled and compromised that it slipped out over the upper lip of the light cover, legs spinning, and fell to the floor. If lizards could be embarrassed, this one would have been. I had that feeling, as I chuckled. But the lizard, not acknowledging my anthropomorphic projections, just ran away expeditiously across the floor and back up a nearby wall, quickly out of my reach.

Tropical and subtropical regions all over our planet contain lots of geckos, in fact over 1,800 species, amounting to more than a quarter of all the world's lizards. But it turns out the species I met is not a native Mexican lizard, but rather an immigrant, originally native to Southeast and South Asia and the Indo-Pacific. It has spread to tropical and subtropical regions on every continent since the age of exploration and more recent extensive global trade. Adding to this confusion among the native lizards of Mexico, yet another immigrant, the Mediterranean house gecko,

Hemidactylus turcicus, has likewise found its way to Mexico. In Mexico and the American tropics, house geckos are known fondly for their value as consumers of the insects that find their way so easily into tropical homes. A popular name saluting this important function is "limpia casa," house cleaner. I have come to know geckos in this context in my travels; they are on watch and on patrol, waiting to devour all manner of tiny flies, mosquitos, little moths, and whatever flies or crawls into a light or otherwise finds its way into any part of a house. Thus it is human habitation where house geckos readily, and usually secretly, blend in so well with nightlife.

Over the last half a millennium the global environment of our human species has become a vastly cosmopolitan place where blending and re-blending has occurred with the migrations of people, cultures, foods, natural resources, and manufactured products. Many of these now-intermingled elements were earlier restricted to single regions, where they had existed or developed over many millennia prior to the modern era of exploration and trade. The Italians did not have tomatoes, the Irish did not have potatoes, nor did the Chinese of Szechuan have chili spices until the old world "discovered" the new world. Nor did the new world gain its beloved coffee until it came from Africa.

Most of our contemporary human population in North and South America consists of immigrants from all corners of Earth who have joined the remaining descendants of American indigenous people. Some of the animals and plants that have been transported to new continents by human conveyance, whether intentional or unintentional, have become recognized in the meantime as invaders or pests. Others are benign and simply accepted, even warmly, by humans who appreciate the full range of the natural world around us.

Getting back to geckos, neither the Mediterranean nor the Asian geckos now living in the western hemisphere are generally considered as invasive pests that require an eradication plan. In fact these two geckos could probably never be eradicated anyway. They are tough, clever, and successful. They are generally welcomed and endeared as members of the local fauna, if not the household itself.

My experience with house geckos in Mexico was a splendidly fun encounter with perfectly natural lizard behavior. It did not occur in the nearby jungle or the dry thorn scrub. It happened in town, in human habitation. But it reminded me that nature is everywhere. We just need to seek it out. We don't have to visit pristine wilderness to witness the results of natural selection. Nor do we have to collect formal scientific data on a population to appreciate how a species fits into its environment. Each light cover in the Mexican apartments was a small-scale ecosystem, brought to life each night by an automatic switch that turned on lights and attracted a sample of living nature to each doorway. I was fortunate to chance upon and discover the joy of this natural phenomenon and to derive a few reflections from the experience.

7

SOMEONE WHO SHOWED ME

LIZARDS AND A FUTURE IN
BIOLOGY

D riving toward Palm Springs on a spring day in 1964, near the end of my freshman year in college, my fellow student comrades and I were not, in fact, escaping for a weekend getaway to the culture of the famous desert resort town. This was, instead, freshman *General Zoology 51b*, led by our young professor, affectionately known as Dr. Mac. The professor had prepared us ahead of time with the fascinating announcement that we would be searching the scorching sands of the lower Mojave Desert among widely spaced creosote bushes to find and capture lizards, specifically the desert iguana, *Dipsosaurus dorsalis*. I had no idea what would actually unfold that day, nor thereafter. But I have since come to realize that the short experience of that day in nature opened a door to the rest of my life.

The world in 1964 was on the brink of change. John F. Kennedy's assassination in the previous autumn had shocked me and fellow college students into an emotional spell, and with the civil rights movement on top of that, our ideals were being stirred. Yet on this beautiful day in the first spring after we lost our young president, here I was heading out into the desert to meet lizards. This was also six years before the first Earth Day, and the ecology movement had not yet taken hold in our society. The essence of this class field trip was all new to me — scientific natural history. What is ecology?

Bleary-eyed college students, on an early Saturday morning, too early, we had boarded a yellow school bus, of the kind used by local public schools, for our eclectic and mysterious academic adventure. Freshman zoology was one of the most popular courses in our small liberal arts college, and zoology was at the time the most popular major. The college dining hall provided brown-bag lunches, and we had also loaded big water jugs for drinking, all stowed beneath the bus. Riding for a couple of hours out of the Los Angeles Basin, we headed up into the San Bernardino Mountains and the half-mile-high pass between Mount San Gorgonio and Mount San Jacinto. Shortly we dropped down into the flat lowlands, with elevations decreasing to only 500 feet as we approached the town of Palm Springs. We looked back up to the west at 10,000-foot, snow-capped Mount San Jacinto. The massive mountain range seemed to wall us off from the coastal province. We were out in the desert!

Simple school buses of the era were not air conditioned, except for the windows we opened. So we felt the warming midmorning desert as we approached our destination, and the bus slowed as it diverted onto a side road and into outlying natural desert terrain. Dr. Mac ordered the bus to a halt, and we got off. As I stepped out, I sensed a surge of hot air against my body, bright reflections of light and radiant energy from the ground around me, and visions of heat shimmering in the tops of bushes and just above the open sandy soil.

With field notebooks in hand, we prepared to mobilize for our mission. Our professor would shortly orient us to our tasks of working in small groups and recording data. He had previously briefed us on the desert iguana, supposedly the biggest lizard in the area. Mature adults could be 15 inches long, including the tail that stretched more than once and a half again the length of just the torso (nose to hips). Being big might make them easier to find, catch, and handle than all those other tiny little lizards. But right now all we could see was just plain desert. The adventure of finding even the first of these supposedly common lizards still awaited us, along with the total mystery of how it would actually happen.

Dr. Mac moved quietly among us as we awaited his instructions. He wore jeans and a common blue work shirt, and desert boots. We wore sneakers, shorts, and t-shirts. Now he prepared to hand out some slender green bamboo canes, limber and about four feet long, that he had freshly cut for our field trip. To the tip of each of these lizard poles he had already fashioned a small noose out of monofilament line, with an opening about the size of a 25-cent piece. This was what I was going to use to catch a lizard, I mused, as I listened attentively to the professor's further instructions: advance slowly toward a motionless individual at its resting spot beneath a creosote bush and lower the noose over the snout and around the neck and then—lift! Dr. Mac's demeanor always conveyed seriousness when science was discussed, but we also sensed fun and humor in the whimsical nature of what he was instructing us to do in the name of science.

It would be no problem to encounter creosote bushes. We could already see them, uncountable, beginning at the side of the road, the Mojave Desert's most common and abundant shrub, mostly three to eight feet tall and forming a seeming monoculture out here. For the lizards, we would just have to head out and start looking. Dr. Mac instructed us further on what to do with a desert iguana, once captured, and before we could release it happily back into its home habitat.

Next he showed us a Schultheiss thermometer—a thin, specially manufactured glass rod, about seven inches long, containing a mercury column and a tip so tiny that it would respond within just a few seconds to provide a reading in degrees Celsius of the lizard's internal body temperature. He described the thermometer's features, carefully holding it in his fingers, one of which carried a silver ring bearing a distinctive turquoise stone. The scale markings on the thermometer ranged from zero (freezing) to 50 degrees Celsius (half the temperature of boiling water), in one-degree increments, and with further tiny lines marking each two-tenths of a degree. This was scientific precision! The main length of the thermometer rod was about three sixteenths of an inch in diameter and three-sided rather than round. The sensitive mercury-filled tip was round and only about a quarter of an inch long, with a diameter that tapered down to only about a sixteenth of an inch.

Of course we could only use the thermometer to obtain lizard body temperature if we knew how to insert the thermometer into an appropriate body orifice. Next instruction. We needed, according to Dr. Mac, to locate the lizard's cloaca and then gently insert the Schultheiss to a depth of about half an inch. Cloaca is the Latin word for sewer, referring to the single body-exit chamber of reptiles. From inside the body the cloaca receives and then ejects, at appropriate times and places, materials that pass out of three separate sets of internal tubes or ducts representing the digestive, urinary, and reproductive systems. That makes reptile plumbing pretty different from our human system and from mammals in general. In desert iguanas, Dr. Mac instructed, we would find the cloacal vent in a swelling at the base of the tail, between the big hind legs. Final instruction: record the temperature and time for each measurement of a freshly captured lizard, as well as any other observation of the lizard's behavior or the environment that might be interesting. Dr. Mac distributed the available thermometers to our teams, and we were off.

Spreading out into the scrub, my partners and I began our pursuit. We worked in teams of three or four students each. Would-be teachers, dentists, doctors, biochemists, biologists, perhaps ecologists, a good mix of both women and men—all our teams were made up of young people who seemed to be taking *Zoology 51b* and Dr. Mac for serious.

The bamboo rod in my hand felt as familiar as a fishing pole, but everything else out here in the desert was new. Hot air seemed hotter all the time, as my body absorbed heat from the sun and the radiant ground below me. I sweated. I felt more comfortable moving than standing still, but where and when would we find our lizard? An acrid smell filled the hot air, and we figured out it was a volatile product from the small but thick and tough, oily-looking leaves of the creosote bush. Rubbing the leaves between my fingers, they became sticky, and the smell of the substance on my fingers was the same as the atmosphere that emanated from the creosote bushes around us. Dainty yellow flowers adorned many of the twigs on the creosote bushes, adding a sweet color to the otherwise rugged and rather dull green shrubs. I liked these bushes.

A sudden bizarre explosion of whirling motion at our feet answered the where-and-when question, as the first desert iguana I'd ever seen in my life launched itself from a nearby creosote bush mound, rearing up on its haunches in *Velociraptor*-like form. It skittered across the surface with shoulders elevated above the ground, propelling itself with alternating strokes of its hind limbs. This is called bipedal ("on two feet") locomotion, quite an impressive display. The lizard's bee-line route shot straight toward a distant creosote mound, where the big white lizard disappeared into a mottled matrix of sunspots and shaded sand among low branches and leaf litter. This stunning surprise revealed to me an animal who was fast, strange, graceful, and beautiful all at the same time.

We would have no trouble detecting iguanas if we just walked around scaring them out of the bushes, but this approach was not going to help us catch them. We determined to adopt Dr. Mac's advice, to move more slowly and quietly, inspecting one creosote mound after another until we spotted a lizard at rest. This took another ten minutes or so, but then we hand-signaled to one another and pointed to an individual parked in the tangle at the base of a bush. The discovery of a motionless lizard, privately concealed, seemed like uncovering secret treasure—a creature unseen by the surrounding desert. Could we now reach in with the bamboo tip to approach the lizard's head? I elected myself to commandeer the pole.

My first fumbling attempt failed, and after that a couple more. A lizard would cock its head toward my standing torso, six or eight feet away, and somehow decide not to flee initially, but then suddenly it would just fire away, out of sight. Another lizard would remain stationary beneath its creosote bush and attentive to the downward-extending pole. It would shake its head at the tickle of the looming noose. And then it might shuffle a few steps away to an impenetrable spot among low-spread branches. I needed to be more patient with these random mismatches of the animal's behavior with our goal of capture. Finally everything lined up to get the loop at the correct angle to encircle the snout and draw back toward the shoulders and then—lift! A kicking, flailing tenth-of-a-pound lizard, heavy on the bent bamboo rod delighted us all, to joyous shouts of "got 'em," as I extended the pole high above the bush and out into the open with the prize dangling above us. Finding nothing to kick against, the lizard became motionless until the first of my friends reached toward the suspended prize.

Wiggling and scratching at approaching human

hands, the gyrating lizard bounced at the tip of the bamboo pole, which seemed to discourage our initial attempts to grab the lizard. The weight of the lizard, restrained by this standard noosing method, was not enough to produce a dangerous constriction around the neck. Again, recalling more of Dr. Mac's pointers, one of my partners made a quick and firm grab with two hands, subduing the head (and its moving jaws) along with the shoulders and hips so that the animal was immobilized. The technique was all a matter of stopping the moving parts from moving and not allowing them to contact surfaces against which they could deliver propulsive thrusts or scratches. With the lizard finally in a secure hold, we easily removed the noose.

The thermometer! Time is of the essence. Quickly another team member brought in the Schultheiss, and we shared words of guidance, up, down, over, and in! Watching the silvery liquid mercury column, we saw that it stabilized within a few seconds, and we fixed our gaze as it remained at the mark. We duly recorded the temperature and time on our clipboard. Squatting gently to the desert floor, the class member holding the lizard reached toward the surface and let go of our first capture, who promptly flew away across the sand in the bipedal sprint that we now watched with such delight. Freedom! The animal paused under a nearby creosote in what I saw as a triumphant stance, its head and shoulders raised above the sand.

Dr. Mac circulated out among the teams and offered his affirmations and helpful suggestions for what we might be doing, how to grasp a lizard more gently, how to insert the thermometer with greater ease and comfort for all concerned. You can hold the lizard in just one hand by securing your thumb and forefinger behind the head, basically grabbing the animal by the scruff of the neck, and then using your other hand to position the hips and base of the tail between your fourth and fifth fingers on the same hand that's securing the lizard's head and neck. For me, the lizard was in my left hand, so I could use my right hand to insert the thermometer. Good to learn how it could became a one-person operation. This all seemed very professional, very scientific. We were serious field herpetologists! Dr. Mac not only congratulated us as we obtained successful temperature readings, he also told us what herpetologists fondly called the method we were using: "noose 'em and goose 'em." Or, he added: "grab 'em and jab 'em!"

We spent the better part of two hours finding and noosing desert iguanas and taking their body temperatures. As we took turns capturing more lizards, the moments in which I held each lizard in my hands became more satisfying. What a noble and handsome beast each one seemed to be. Still and quiet once secured in my hands, always with the seemingly knowing eye looking up at me, these were beautiful creatures. To the touch, the desert iguana's skin was smooth, and its scales were small, unlike those of other lizards with large, rough, shingle-like scales. I liked the smoothness of the iguana's skin against the palm of my hand and my index finger, which I used to stroke the lizard's lower back and tail. One facet of the lizard's body surface that contrasted with the small smooth body scales was a single row of enlarged scales beginning on the center line at the back of the head and running along the spine. In fact these magnificent back-crest scales were a mini-version of the big spikes that run along the backs of giant tropical iguanas.

Finally we all assembled back at the bus to contribute our numbers to a pool of data. Dr. Mac organized us to produce a summary. The values of internal body temperature in lizards that we found by late morning and midday mostly fell in the range of 40 to 44 degrees Celsius, which amounts to 104 to 111 degrees Fahrenheit. It was immediately and strikingly obvious that this was well above the human body temperature benchmark of 98.6 Fahrenheit (37 Celsius). We had all gained the vivid impression that our lizards were both lively and hot, first from their vigorous movements as we attempted to subdue them and secondly from the hot sensation of their skin against ours. These were anything but lethargic "cold-blooded" animals.

Our basic physiology lesson here was that the body temperature of active desert iguanas exceeded our own human body temperature. All of us were impressed, including the many pre-medical students in the class, who were highly intent on understanding human physiology, certainly more so than lizard physiology. The pre-meds were of course also highly intent on getting into medical school. Perhaps the superiority of lizard body temperature to that of humans was a disappointment for some of the pre-meds—a deflation of the primacy of the human species. Is there something better about lizards than humans? My own feeling was that the hot body temperature of lizards was near the top of the list of all the novelties and curiosities to which I was introduced as a freshman. In fact, this was profound. We should not be thinking about reptiles as cold-blooded. The cold-blooded epithet has been used to label animals without sufficiently powerful metabolism to generate the high and relatively constant body temperatures that characterize mammals and birds. Instead, reptiles expose themselves to environmental conditions like bright sunshine and hot soil or rock surfaces that help them to heat up their bodies. A better name for the physiology of these kinds of animals that acquire body heat from the environment is ectothermy, Dr. Mac informed us, literally referring to heat coming from an outside source.

What about their speed, now that we had learned that the lizards were so hot? How fast were they? The hotter, the faster, one could imagine by simple physical laws. It turns out that a herpetologist named Belkin, who wanted to learn how fast lizards could run, actually spent some time right out here in the desert near Palm Springs in the 1950s pursuing desert iguanas with a stop watch and a measuring tape. He followed their tracks in the sand after he measured a start and stop time and then measured the distance between the beginning and ending points of the sprint. He measured straight-line speed courses on twenty-three lizards that he was able to startle into running away. His published measurements averaged 7.3 meters per second, with a maximum of just over 8 meters per second, which is about 18 miles per hour. This is faster than we typically ride our bicycles. Lizards are pretty fast!

As I stepped back up into the bus, I felt very satisfied that I had held wild desert lizards in my hand. This was an animal whose beauty I first saw as it ran across the desert toward a creosote bush mound and then rested beneath the bush. Then I felt its hot skin against my hand and received the look of the lizard's eye back at me as I gazed at the wonder resting in my hand. I was pleased with the rewarding connection I had made with lizards and creosote bushes. It took a professor's effort and commitment to organize a group of students to experience this desert adventure. And Dr. Mac was the one who took me there.

After lunch we had a little free time to roam the main street of Palm Springs, and then we re-boarded the bus, where Dr. Mac announced the plan for the rest of the afternoon. He was taking us to the base of nearby Mount San Jacinto to look for an unusual lizard. The professor directed the bus up a windy road into Chino Canyon. Rock walls, massive boulders, and rocks of all sizes surrounded the roadway leading up the big mountain. This was a cornucopia of rocks. We had yet to hear Dr. Mac's explanation of what was special about this lizard, assuming that we could find one. For starters, it was called the banded rock lizard, which matched the abundance of rocks we could see out the bus's window. More amusing Latin emerged from Dr. Mac: *Streptosaurus mearns*i, quite a name for a lizard.

A turn-out shelf along the winding road provided

our opportunity to stop. We got out of the bus and prepared to explore the rocky mountain side. With our climb in altitude up the mountain road, we had moved into a cooler air mass, and a gentle breeze added to the cooling effect. We looked down to the desert flats below. Based on our morning's experience down below, we already felt like veteran herpetologists, as we awaited Dr. Mac's distribution of the bamboo poles. He instructed us to search the vertical rock walls, the cracks in the rocks, and the smaller rock fragments that formed loose caps on top of some of the corroding old boulders that awaited us nearby. The lizards would either be perched in places where they could grab passing insects, or they would just be out basking in the sun to assist their digestion of bugs captured earlier.

Before we fanned out on our search, Dr. Mac explained that one of the unusual things about these lizards was their association with big rocks, used both as perches and as shelter. Herpetologists in fact have seen this lizard only rarely on the ground. Then he added that this population was also unusual on a geographic scale because all the rest of the comrades of this species lived in abundance further to the south, extending down through the northern half of the Baja California peninsula. In other words, up here in southern California's lower Mojave Desert country, we were hoping to find the very northernmost individuals belonging to this species. In the parlance of biogeography, the population here was located at the northern range margin of a specialized rock-dwelling lizard that was otherwise only found in Mexico.

Dr. Mac repeated, for those of us who were curious about the scientific name: *Streptosaurus mearnsi*. I liked the Latin names that Dr. Mac uttered so matter-of-factly. This was science. After the early 1960s, herpetologists changed the Latin name further to *Petrosaurus mearnsi*, by which *"petro"* (rock, stone) does justice to the rock lizard named after Dr. Edgar Alexander Mearns, early twentieth-century naturalist. Such were the rewards for the naturalists of old.

Quite a distinguished fellow, Mearns was invited by Teddy Roosevelt on his expedition to Africa to collect specimens for the Smithsonian Institution, which was just opening up its new natural history museum.

Enough orientation to the rock lizard. We were ready to rumble out into the boulders. The steep, rocky terrain was inviting us to climb up and among the stone masses. Looking around at so much rockery and upward to the top of the mountain gave me the impression that these dynamic rocks had broken off of the massive mountain above and were in the process of following gravity toward the desert below. The terrain evoked a sense of exploration, and fun. We were attracted to the rocks, nice to touch, rough and warm, hotter on their sunny sides. It was not long until shouts and waves began to signal that various groups were finding lizards. My group brought our first capture down to Dr. Mac. Happily we received his approval and positive identification that we had found the banded rock lizard! This was a handsome reptile, with a pronounced dark collar or ring around its neck, just in front of the shoulders. And a striking pattern on the tail: broad bands of dark color alternating with the light general body color all the way to the tip of the tail. The rock lizard was smaller than the desert iguana and also rather flat-bodied, making it well suited for clinging to rocks, not at all as rotund and corpulent as its bigger cousin the herbivorous desert iguana of the creosote flats.

Dr. Mac slipped our rock lizard into a small cotton cloth bag with a draw-string closure, allowing the animal to quiet down. We carried the bagged lizard back where we'd found it. I held the squirming bag in my hand and then made a firm hold on the lizard's torso from outside the bag. At that point one of my partners loosened the drawstring on the bag, and we allowed the lizard's head to emerge. I lowered it to the top of a boulder and let go. The lizard seemed to wait quietly for a moment, as if reorienting to the world from which it had been snatched by strange intruders.

A few seconds later it scampered away across the boulder and disappeared into a crack in the rock face.

 We had a great time spotting a few more of these wonderful critters on the rocks. We mostly just observed them, out of our reach, resting or perhaps scuttling across big rock faces. Something that thrilled me about grabbing a lizard was watching its head, so noble and attentive, and then the look of the eye, moving in its socket, somehow letting me know that the lizard was regarding me as I regarded it. Through our short time among the boulders and the lizards, I think I formed an emotional bond with both the rocky realm of the canyon and its resident lizards. It felt good to be on a mountainside on the same day we'd spent earlier in sandy flats below. Somehow in the exhilaration I also embraced the biological insight that I was personally meeting up with the northernmost individuals on the planet that belonged to an otherwise Mexican species of lizard. Nations, states and provinces, and counties can all be proud of their biodiversity make-up, however rich that may be. Although we often meet a widespread species somewhere in the middle of its geographic range, it can be especially rewarding to encounter a rare individual who is a member of a geographically extreme population, such as this northernmost population of banded rock lizards.

 We returned to the college by the end of the afternoon, but the Saturday night campus social atmosphere did not erase the powerful impressions I gained from this remarkable freshman day in the desert. Catching and holding lizards in my hands. Feeling their lively hot bodies and wiggling legs. Letting them go back where they belonged. Touching oily and smelly creosote bush leaves. I wondered about creosote bushes and desert iguanas as co-inhabitants of the desert ecosystem. The creosote bush served needs of the desert iguana. Did the iguana do anything for the creosote? It seemed like a strong association, a partnership perhaps.

Creosote bushes seem to have something of a monopoly out in the desert sands of California and nearby Nevada, Arizona, and northwestern Mexico. This monopoly of magnificence and ecological domination springs from the evolutionary success of the creosote bush. The bushes are widely spaced, and most of the ground between them appears bare and open. Below these open spaces and at shallow depths, the roots of mature creosote bushes radiate beyond the centric soil mound of each bush. The shallow roots pull in water quickly, before it can evaporate, from the rare, periodic precipitations that fall on the desert. The small tough leaves are only about a quarter to three eighths of an inch long and formed in tiny pairs along the thinner twigs on the woody branches. The bright buttercup-yellow flowers have five tiny petals, only about a quarter of an inch long. Herpetologists have observed desert iguanas eating both the leaves and the petals of creosote bushes, as well as young buds and the mature fruits that develop from the flowers. That requires behavior I did not get to observe on my inaugural day of desert iguana observation. Desert iguanas actually climb up into these bushes to feed, getting up to six feet or more above the ground. Besides food, the creosote provides refuge to desert iguanas, not only the protective matrix of basal branches that is impenetrable to some kinds of predators, but the stable soil mound at the base. The mounds contain underground retreats, burrows that are more often dug originally by desert rodents than by the iguanas themselves.

Once you've been out among the creosote bushes and seen desert iguanas living in their midst, the relationship seems obvious. But the association does not explain how and why they fit together. An important feature of creosote bush leaves, flowers, buds and fruits is simply their abundance. Lots of bushes, lots of food, and easy to find for desert iguanas. So, the dominating abundance of creosote bushes is a big part of the ready provisioning of desert iguanas with their basic diet.

I came to admire these two co-habitating desert organisms that have remained icons for me ever since that spring day of my freshman year—the desert iguana and the creosote bush. I would discover more about them in the next few years with further experience in the Mojave Desert. I would meet a herpetology professor in graduate school who had studied the desert iguana himself as a graduate student. In fact, I spent an entire springtime, several years later, taking that professor's field course in herpetology, with a huge dedication of time tracking down lizards and snakes across the Mojave Desert. The next few years ahead of me would provide an abundance of opportunities to know nature better by engaging my senses in the desert world.

Back on campus in the zoology lecture hall we had a few more meetings of Dr. Mac's course to finish up the semester. The professor always arrived early and prepared previews of the day's material on the blackboard using colored chalk to make attractive drawings. I remember distinctly the morning when he carefully drew the heads of four different species of finches, each with a conspicuously different beak shape. These were the finches illuminated by Charles Darwin, four species of the genus *Geospiza* that Dr. Mac selected from an iconic illustration of the evolutionary radiation and divergence, out on the Galapagos Archipelago, of a group of ground finches derived from ancestors from the South American mainland. I especially liked Dr. Mac's drawing of the one with the biggest and thickest beak, *magnirostris*, or big beak. I copied the shapes of the beaks and the Latin names of all four species faithfully into my notebook. This was evolution, explained by the mechanism that began with mutations that resulted in slight differences that gradually became bigger differences, due to natural selection, all working together to generate new species. Dr. Mac played the important role of launching my interest in the academic world of evolutionary biology, the great theme that unifies all of biology. So goes the famous statement of T. Dobzhansky: "Nothing in biology makes sense except in light of evolution."

Looking back now at my far-away and long-ago freshman year in college, I know that I experienced a powerful attraction to the desert—it seemed at the time to be all about lizards, bushes, and sandy soil. But I've come to realize more and more in the passing years how deeply it was that Dr. Mac himself impressed me in that short period of time. His good-natured manner, his dedication to his students, and his own love of nature all captured me. I always sensed that he was having fun too, being a professor and a scientist. He showed me a way of engaging with the natural world that carried on through my own life.

What I didn't realize at the time was that the experiences Dr. Mac offered me were the beginnings of my own life as a biology professor in pursuit of scientific natural history. In the spring of 1964, I could only make a brief, initial response to the thrill of lizards and creosote bushes. I liked them. I also began to hear good words on campus about Dr. Mac's very popular *Animal Ecology* course, and indeed I would enroll in that the following spring. A field course, more field trips! Dr. Mac was an example and a model. He turned up at an important moment in my early life trajectory and pointed me toward something good. He was someone who showed me. Perhaps we should look back more often to long-ago experiences in order to figure out what happened then that made us what we are now.

8

MEETING KANGAROO RATS AND DESERTS

nimal Ecology was the course name I spotted, and the college catalog description for *Zoology 157* in the spring semester of 1965 grabbed me even more with the promise of desert animals, field trips, and a small class limited to only twenty. I was thrilled to receive permission to enroll from the professor, who had taken me the previous spring as a freshman out into California's Mojave Desert to meet lizards on a field trip with the introductory zoology course. I decided I wanted more desert and more of the critters who mysteriously managed to live under the desert's harsh extremes of heat, aridity, and scarcity of resources.

As a sophomore I declared zoology to be my major, and I don't recall what else I had to tell Dr. Mac in order to gain a place in his ecology class of mostly juniors and seniors, but it worked. We were destined to learn about "environment, communities, populations, distribution, and evolution," to quote directly from the catalog. But those academic abstractions would only come to life for me in the field, on field trips, out in the sand and rocks, the scrubby bushes, and the cactus. Dr. Mac and his course had developed a strong word-of-mouth reputation around the college. He was listed in the catalog as an assistant professor who joined the college in 1960, suggesting that he had quickly become popular. In fact, the college had already acknowledged his popularity by giving him their annual distinguished professor award. His home address, on College Avenue, on the edge of campus, was also listed in the catalog for our convenience. This was the culture of small, liberal arts colleges at the time.

In the spring of 1965 the US had just begun its ground offensive in Viet Nam. I, like other students of the era, had serious concerns about Viet Nam and the future of our country on my mind. For now, finding the best things to do while still enrolled in college seemed right—exploring any door that academia might open to me. Although I didn't know it at the start of the semester, Dr. Mac was going to acquaint me first-hand with three of North America's major deserts: the Mojave, the Sonoran, and the Great Basin. And I would meet some of the most remarkable little mammals in the world: kangaroo rats, who quickly became my personal favorites. I was in the process of becoming entranced by nature. I didn't realize that I was embarking on a formative experience that would shape the rest of my life.

Our first field trip, on a Friday afternoon, was a short late-afternoon jaunt within half an hour of campus. We drove, in cars belonging to students, along a paved county road and pulled off onto a short dirt track that dead-ended in a plot of scrubby vegetation. We got out and shuffled around on the gravelly ground, among occasional big boulders and open spots of sandy soil. We were on an alluvial fan at the foot of southern California's San Gabriel

Mountains. These mountains bound the interior side of the Los Angeles Basin. The earlier natural landscape of the L.A. Basin used to be largely this same mix of coastal sage scrub and chaparral, recognized ecologically as a semidesert. Because I was also taking introductory geology, I had just learned about alluvial fans—sediments deposited in the shape of a fan by streams that erode mountains down to their base. We were looking up at 10,080-foot Mount San Antonio from our site in the mouth of San Antonio Canyon, and Dr. Mac explained that we were standing on deposits brought down by rains and the natural flow of San Antonio Creek.

At the end of a warm day of bright sunshine the air was filled with pungent smells released from the vegetation—bushes such as the two species of sagebrush (*Artemisia*, in the sunflower family) and two species of true sage (*Salvia*, in the mint family) and from the bigger chaparral bushes, laurel sumac and lemonadeberry, up to 25 feet tall. As Dr. Mac named each species, my attention to the plants was heightened because I was also taking a botany course on the diversity of southern California's flora. A lot was going on to attract my attention out here!

Dr. Mac had plenty to tell us about the area's ecology, including the geology and botany, because this was where he had conducted his own PhD research on the populations of seven nocturnal rodent species that lived together in this community. It surprised me to hear that so many species (mice and rats of various kinds) could live in one local piece of habitat. Dr. Mac wanted us to meet this whole diverse array of rodents. We were going to set out live traps and come back the next morning to find out who was in each trap. To each group of two or three students, Dr. Mac assigned a box containing a couple dozen small aluminum box traps. Each trap had a hinged, fold-down door that could be latched down with a catch on a treadle that would release and close the door when the rodent stood on the floor at the back of the trap to pick up the seed bait (just common bird-food seed) that we threw into the trap. He walked us out along some open spaces where we could place the traps in loops or lines so we could find them the next morning. The traps were all numbered consecutively to make it easy to keep track of each line, and we set out about 200 traps.

The sun was dropping low to the west as we finished baiting the traps. Cool air flowing down the canyon met us as we stood among boulders still warm with the heat of the day. We drove back to the college for a typical Friday night of campus life, got some sleep, and returned early the next morning with anticipation.

Each team dispersed to walk its trap line, instructed by Dr. Mac to bring back the closed traps so we could all examine the contents together. I recall the excitement of the first closed door, and the second, and more. Picking up a trap sometimes elicited scratching or sliding sounds from within. Usually the trap was just quiet, perhaps a little mouse hunkering down inside, equally curious about who was outside. Rarely any audible vocalizations, as nocturnal rodents don't usually communicate in our frequency range. Tilting the trap usually produced a sound from left-over seeds rolling across the bottom. I couldn't resist pushing down slightly to open the door a bit, but it was hard to look in through the little crack, since the door still mostly blocked the view of the creature inside. Perhaps the animal jumped up at the crack in the doorway. It seemed better to take it easy and wait, so the critter would not escape, and just see how the professor would handle this.

As we handed our traps to Dr. Mac, we watched his recommended ways of examining the rodents. His every move seemed confident, and he was completely at ease, as he chatted about the animals and their habitat differences, diets, and behaviors. Holding the trap vertically, he pressed the door downward, on its springed hinge to open his view toward the animal down in the bottom. He seemed to be able to tell whether or not the little animal was going to jump out, or perhaps run up his shirt sleeve, or whether it would just sit in the back of the trap. For some of the quiet little mice, he just reached his hand inside and cupped the creature into his fingers and the palm of his hand. Some of the bigger or more actively moving rodents he transferred into a clear glass jar with a diameter very similar to the rectangular opening at the end of the trap; then he slipped a screw-top lid onto the jar. Holes in the lid allowed air exchange, and the glass walls allowed us to see the animal's size, physical features, and coloration. Dr. Mac handled all the animals easily and gently with his bare hands, and because he was so at-ease with the animals, each little rodent seemed to be a pleasant and attractive creature.

Of three species of common little brown or grayish deer mice (*Peromyscus*), all six inches or so in length (including tail) and weighing more or less an ounce, Dr. Mac, pointed out differences in their tails, ears, body size, and coloration that allowed identification. Much bigger, at about a foot long and weighing a third to nearly half a pound (and found in the traps that felt heavy when we picked them up), were the fascinating woodrats, or packrats (*Neotoma*) of two species. Dr. Mac showed us their above-ground "houses," which were piles of dead twigs, cactus bits, and stones that the rats gathered and fashioned into shelters that protected them from both physical elements and predators. Some of the packrat houses were actually constructed in and around living cactus plants. He explained that the legendary name of the packrat and its behavior are related to the predilection of these rodents for rummaging around to gather objects of any kind to contribute to the structural magnificence of their houses. The soft fur and bristling whiskers and the big eyes of these large rodents appealed to me, as an indication of a good, wild rodent with a gentle life style. The woodrats, explained Dr. Mac, consumed a great deal of green cactus pulp, providing them with both nutrition and water. He showed us prickly pear cactus plants that had been extensively chewed by the woodrats. The smaller and more common species was the desert woodrat (*Neotoma lepida*) and the larger and less common was the dusky-footed woodrat (*Neotoma fuscipes*). Taken together, the three species of deer mice and two species of woodrats belong to the same rodent family that contains the most common and abundant wild rodents that are spread throughout the entire North American continent in every kind of habitat.

Early along, after we had examined only the first few traps, Dr. Mac opened one trap that drew a collective "wow" as we crowded around and he announced "kangaroo rat!" This was the pacific kangaroo rat, *Dipodomys agilis*, a Latin suggestion of agility, which I liked. The genus name *Dipodomys* indicated a two-footed (*dipod*) mouse (*mys*), referring to the enormous gangly hind feet (about an inch and a half long) on the little rat, similar in proportion to the big feet of a hopping kangaroo.

Dr. Mac explained the connection of the rodent's "kangaroo" name to locomotion. This little two-ounce rodent, with an oversized head, a body about four or more inches long, and a tail nearly once and a half again that long, was capable of bipedal (two-foot) hopping, which we got to see a few minutes later when Dr. Mac set the animal down on the ground. It remained still momentarily, groomed itself a bit with its tiny front paws, rubbed its shoulders and flanks in the sand, stood steadily again, and then launched itself off like a shot across a short space of open terrain, with its long, stiffened tail wavering behind as a counterbalance to each simultaneous downward thrust of both its powerful hind legs that propelled the animal forward in leaps of three feet or more in length. With this live demonstration of bipedal speed-hopping, we saw how the little animal that initially looked so funny because of its entirely disproportionate body (by general mouse standards) could be such an effective locomotory travelling machine.

While still in Dr. Mac's hands, the first kangaroo rat I had ever seen in my life served for Dr. Mac's adept demonstration of various of its remarkable features, starting with the huge head, that appeared to be nearly half the length of the body, and big eyes. The big skull was further exaggerated by the stuffed cheek pouches on the sides of the head, extending back along the neck; the rat had crammed its pouches with the abundant supply of seeds that we'd thrown into the trap. Kangaroo rat cheek pouches, unlike those of squirrels and many other rodents, are not cheeky extensions inside the mouth or throat. The kangaroo rat's cheek pouches, one on each side of the body, are separate from the mouth and lined with fur, just like the fur on the outside of the body, but shorter. Dr. Mac showed us this by holding the rat gently by the scruff of its neck between his thumb and forefinger and poking gently with fingers of the other hand at the bulge on the side of the head, then pulling out a little pinch of the soft and flexible cheek skin on one side to expose the opening just behind the corner of the mouth. Pulling further, he widened the natural opening so we could see the seeds and the fur lining inside the pouch. I was amazed!

The kangaroo rat, still held by the scruff of its neck in Dr. Mac's hand, next did what I later learned was typical of a kangaroo rat in the hand. It began pushing with its front paws from back to front along both sides of its face to eject dozens of seeds from its pouches. Somehow in this compromised situation, the rat was provoked to jettison its cheek-pouch cargo, which spilled to the ground at our feet like coins bursting out of a Las Vegas slot machine. To load the pouches in the first place, the rat, sitting in the trap last night, had bypassed its mouth with the seeds held in its paws and tucked them, instead, backward into the waiting fur-lined pockets. Kangaroo rats can productively gather a lot of seeds while out on the surface at night, without having to take time to ingest, chew, and swallow until they get back into the underground safety of their burrows, where they might also choose to cache any surplus from the night's harvest.

This strange little animal, so extreme, so unexpectedly bizarre must have been a big part of what was putting me into a trance of enthusiasm for life in the desert. Everything I saw about the kangaroo rat was new and totally believable, and I was overwhelmed that one kind of rodent could be so different and so charming, compared to the plain gray house mouse that my mother and I watched in shock as it jumped out of a kitchen cupboard when I was six years old.

After a few more traps we found a little mouse, brownish in color and with a long tail, immediately identified by Dr. Mac as the San Diego pocket mouse, now known as *Chaetodipus fallax* — a smaller member of the same family to which kangaroo rats belong. The common name "pocket mouse" refers to its fur-lined cheek pouches, a feature shared by all members of the family. The Latin family name, Heteromyidae, refers to other ("hetero-") mice, meaning simply various other mice. I have continued, over many years now, to understand and appreciate these rodents as "other" — definitely not your usual rats and mice.

I had yet to learn the full story of the magnificent evolutionary success of North America's unique desert rodent family, the Heteromyidae, and how they have succeeded in such great numbers with their nocturnal life style in the arid landscapes of western North America. This region contains about 50 different species of kangaroo rats and pocket mice, all superbly specialized for life in the desert.

We concluded our morning on the alluvial fan among the shrubs, rocks, and cactus by reviewing Dr. Mac's introduction to the semidesert habitat and its resident rodent community — amazing to me that so many different kinds of rodents were living in this one common patch of scrub. We released all the animals, taking our numbered traps back to the spots where they fit in sequence on each line. We enjoyed watching each little creature walk, run or hop back into the brush or enter a burrow that we presumed could be its home. I was impressed with kangaroo rats and Dr. Mac and the trapping routine he'd shown us. With the images of all the bushes, cactus, boulders, and gravel substrate fresh in mind and the fragrant smells of the morning air, I was touched by the beauty of this natural place—beauty that was all the more remarkable when I realized we were right at the edge of southern California's burgeoning urban sprawl.

We were ready for our first overnight field trip, an escape from the Los Angeles Basin by passing northward over the San Gabriel Mountains to camp out on the western fringe of the Mojave Desert, only a short couple of hours away. Besides leaving campus life behind, we were fleeing the human hoards of Los Angeles and the heavily polluted air mass that hung over the L. A. Basin in that era. Cajon Pass, uphill from San Bernardino, provided our route over the mountains, and after crossing over to the back we moved westward along the lower shoulder of the mountains. As we descended into desert country we recognized the brilliant signature wildflower of the Mojave and official state flower, the California poppy that cast its rich golden hues against the drab desert floor. Down in the desert flats, we arrived at our destination, Piute Butte, about 15 miles east of the small towns of Lancaster and Palmdale. (Despite the disrespectful misspelling of the Paiute Native American tribal name, the old spelling of the name unfortunately continues in use on contemporary maps and rosters of geographic places.) We found ourselves joyously on a wild piece of land with no other people around and no facilities of any kind. We jumped out to explore the desert in the late afternoon sun.

I was impressed with the soft, fine sand, and its abundance, and the big open spaces among the bushes. I picked up the sand in my fingers and let it trickle to the ground. Piute Butte itself was old corroding granite, hard to the touch but crumbly. The butte was a great rock mass surrounded by smaller chunks, big boulders really, the size of cars and people. It was a shelter and a landmark, rising up out of sandy surroundings. The big rock conveyed a sense of welcome and protection for us to stay and camp next to its base. It was especially inviting to walk in among the boulders. Some were separated by vertical spaces too close to allow passage while others offered the opportunity to slip in and hide.

As we gathered around and sought out Dr. Mac for his explanations, he began with the two biggest and most conspicuous plants surrounding us — the creosote bush and the Joshua tree. Creosote (*Larrea divaricata*) was generally recognized as the most widespread shrub across the expanse of the Mojave Desert, with tiny thick leaves and bright yellow miniature flowers. This bush already held a fond familiarity for me from my freshman year on Dr. Mac's lizard-catching field trip to the southern Mojave in introductory zoology.

The Joshua tree (*Yucca brevifolia*) was the only thing around that deserved the name "tree," as the tallest of all the yucca species, standing up to 30 or 40 feet. None of the Joshua tree's relatives in the agave family is considered a tree, but all share the same large white showy flowers. Young Joshua trees have long spiny leaves growing on their trunks, but those leaves eventually drop off of the lower, older part of the trunk, leaving rough, dark-colored bark on the older trees. The straight, spine-tipped leaves, from six to twelve inches long, are similar in form to the spear-like leaves of all the other yuccas, but shorter. Interesting, I thought, that the larger species, Joshua tree, has shorter leaves than those on the smaller-sized yucca species. The branches of Joshua trees extend, bending upwards from the main trunk and resembling arms, giving the appearance of giant awkward people. Mormon settlers in the old west imagined these big plants as the prophet Joshua, indicating with out-stretched arms the way to the promised land. Dr.

Mac also quickly explained the difference between two main kinds of cactus we could see around the butte: prickly pear (with big flat pads) and cholla (with long, narrow cylindrical joints).

Dr. Mac issued all the needed commands, in his cheery and welcoming voice, to get us organized for our trapping mission, the same routine he had shown us back on the other side of the mountains. We got right to it and followed his suggestion that some of us should streak out across the sand and creosote, while others should work in among the boulders around the butte. He was clearly setting us up to pay attention to habitat differences. He hinted that the two species of kangaroo rats expected here were mainly going to be out in the open, with burrows beneath creosote bush hillocks and other dune humps. Desert woodrats, in contrast, might be concentrated around the butte's boulders, and as we went around setting traps we should be on the lookout for piles of stones, cactus bits, and old dead twigs built up within boulder crevices and on ledges. These material heaps were—as we had seen in the coastal sage scrub and chaparral—the long-term construction and maintenance projects of woodrats: their houses, containing a well-protected nest somewhere down inside! We saw that many of the cactus, especially the pads of prickly pear, had various gnawing patterns (missing pieces) in them, made by the desert woodrat, the known perpetrator. Cactus serves two roles for woodrats: protective and insulative structural material for the house and a year-round source of water and nutrition. It seemed to me that woodrats deserve credit for turning something often ill-thought-of into a double bonus.

Dr. Mac explained to us that the two new kangaroo rat species we would find here were, in fact, the two most commonly found throughout the entire Mojave Desert and distinct from the agile Pacific kangaroo rat species we'd met on the other side of the mountains. The desert woodrat here at Piute Butte, on the other hand, was going to be the same species we had already seen on the other side of the mountain, reflecting its flexibility to occupy different habitats and life zones, and with a correspondingly greater westward and coastally oriented geographic range. Dr. Mac further suggested that out in the creosote and sand we should also look for woodrat houses next to old fallen-down Joshua trees.

With all the traps set and baited and the sun soon to set, we busied ourselves setting up camp, working on dinner preparations, gathering firewood, and continuing to explore around the butte. Everyone had packed a small bag of personal gear, a sleeping bag, and a ground cloth. My ground cloth was an old worn-out bedspread that did a good job keeping the sand out of my sleeping bag. Dr. Mac had arranged all the food with the college dining hall, whose manager pleased Dr. Mac greatly by providing a big package of steaks to grill over the campfire, along with plenty of bread, salad materials, and provisions for the other meals. The stoves and lanterns, kitchenware, ice chests, and big water jugs were all part of the zoology department's field gear.

I explored the area a bit more on my own in the cooling air. I was quite taken by the gigantic crumbly old granite rocks. Walking among these giants, it felt good to place the palm of my hand against the warm, rough surfaces, rubbing them and releasing crumbs from the rock mass. The material at the base of the rocks was these old granite bits, degraded by sun and wind and occasional water, and by time. Looking in on a shaded horizontal shelf in a big crack between two adjoining boulders, I spotted an array of sticks, cactus, and a few small pieces of granite—the home of a woodrat! Large black fecal pellets, with an unusual and not necessarily ratty odor, were strewn around at the front of the ledge. Walking further I noticed small drifts of fine sand that had blown in against the rock here and there on the windward side of boulders.

The evening passed quickly and was obviously a time of jollity, singing, joke telling, and gossip covering a full range of topics: fellow students, college social issues, professors and their expertise, boredom, kindness, generosity, pomposity, and every other imaginable personality trait. Guitars accompanied campfire music, and new songs had to be taught and learned by repetition, with the chance they might come back on the next field trip.

Next morning Dr. Mac, as one might expect, was the first up. As we stirred, we heard pumping sounds from the tank on the Coleman stove, in preparation for making cowboy coffee, as Dr. Mac called it — coffee grounds thrown into boiling water in a large metal pot. The ritualistic secrets of making potable coffee, as the professor revealed, were to extinguish the burner immediately upon dumping in the grounds, then to stir the brew briefly, and finally to add a splash of cold water to make the grounds sink to the bottom, thereby making the coffee less gritty. We grabbed the hot, richly aromatic coffee and some breakfast and socialized around our encampment as part of the waking-up process. Shortly we became anxious to see what our traps would contain. The bright morning sun let us know that the coolness of fresh morning air would not last long, and that gave us a boost to get out and retrieve the traps with doors that had sprung shut during the night.

It was time to meet the two promised kangaroo rats that Dr. Mac was featuring here, along with the woodrats and some other mice. As we brought in the closed traps, some heavy and some light, we crowded around as Dr. Mac pulled the animals out to make introductions. He also encouraged us to go ahead, following his example, to remove the animals on our own. Right away came Merriam's kangaroo rat (*Dipodomys merriami*), unmistakably familiar as a kangaroo rat, with big head, big eyes, big hind feet, and super-long tail. Merriam's was a bit smaller than the pacific kangaroo rat we'd met on the other side of the mountain, and its coloration was much lighter, with light tan on its back and sides together with the pure white underside fur that all kangaroo rats possess. Merriam's tail was a good

6 inches long and contained a fringe of long, darker colored hairs over its distal half. We reviewed cheek pouches again and marveled at the greatly expanded size of the cheeks and faces of several individuals who we imagined might have stuffed their pouches full of additional bait seed that they robbed from out in front of one or more traps before getting caught inside.

The second kangaroo rat species was stunning for its size, gigantic within the kangaroo rat clan and weighing three times as much as Merriam's, at about a quarter of a pound! Its general body coloration was similar to Merriam's—a match to the light background color of desert sand. The body was about five to five and a half inches long, the hind feet were huge, at two inches long, and the tail, heavy and thick, was nearly nine inches long including the beautiful tuft of long hairs at the tip. The long fringe hairs over most of the distal half of the tail were black but changed to a pure white tip over the last inch or so of the tail. This handsome hulk of a kangaroo rat was the desert kangaroo rat (*Dipodomys deserti*), with both common and Latin names appropriately saluting where we were: the desert. This, in my mind, was the ultimate desert rat! The powerful stroke of its massive thigh muscles and explosive thrust of the feet kicking in the air, as Dr. Mac held the animal by the scruff of its neck in his hand, were a signal that this kangaroo rat could be a bit harder to handle than all the other, smaller rodents we had met so far. I learned in the meantime to keep the legs out in free air when holding a kangaroo rat by the scruff of the neck. With nothing to kick against, the animal settles right down and remains quiet in your hand.

As we examined the two kangaroo rat species together at the same time, Dr. Mac showed us another feature shared by these two prime players of the Mojave. He pointed to the long toes on the hind feet of both species, and we counted four toes in both species, all four about the same size and with a little claw at the tip of each. Missing, he remarked, was the fifth toe, which surprised me. But this was a story of evolution in progress. Most of the other twenty or so species of kangaroo rats have five toes on each hind foot, including the pacific kangaroo rat that we'd already met on our first trip. Fast-running mammals of many different kinds have shown the tendency to evolve longer limb bones and to reduce the number of individual bones across the breadth of the legs and feet—lost in evolutionary time—even as remaining bones become longer. This is familiar in the famous story of the evolution of horses, zebras and their relatives (long leg and foot bones but only one big toe, or hoof) and of antelopes, deer, and their relatives (long legs and only two big toes). We concluded from this historical pattern that the desert and Merriam's kangaroo rats, with only four toes on their hind feet, were among the most advanced species of kangaroo rats in adapting to high-speed bipedal running for escape from predators and routine commuting around the desert—all part of their response to the challenges of survival in wide-open desert spaces.

As expected, we caught quite a few desert woodrats around the boulders where we had spotted their houses yesterday, but we also caught some out in the sandy flats, where they had constructed their cactus-stick-stone houses around creosote bush mounds or against old fallen Joshua tree trunks. The big difference in shelter between kangaroo rats and woodrats was that kangaroo rat burrows that provided protection from both desert heat and predators were excavated down in the safety of the soil, whereas woodrats insulated their houses and protected themselves from coyotes and desert foxes by the sheer volume of prickly cactus, sticks, and stones that they assembled into a house-pile located *above* the ground.

As some of us walked with Dr. Mac to check out a woodrat house built around an old dead Joshua tree, we picked through the decomposing bark and turned over a chunk of the trunk. Surprise! A lizard, the yucca night lizard.

The slender, grayish-brown little creature that we had disrupted in its shelter moved slowly, and Dr. Mac easily picked it up to demonstrate and explain a bit about its natural history. It was only about four inches long including the tail. These little lizards were misnamed as "night" lizards, only because they are so secretive in their daytime movements in the decomposing litter that early observers thought they were hiding and waiting to come out at night. They feast mostly on small insects and spiders that inhabit the decaying matter of Joshua trees and other yuccas or bigger desert plants.

Most everyone was becoming comfortable with the rodent trapping and handling procedure on this second trip. I thought it was a terrific routine, and quite professional, something for me to adopt. We dutifully strode back to our trap lines and released the animals near where we caught them. Each release of a kangaroo rat was a small adventure, watching the animal depart in one direction or another, eventually entering an entrance hole into a burrow. We wanted to know where each one lived and wondered if the hole it entered was the actual home, or just the first conveniently available spot where it was able to get back into the safe underground for daytime rest. Of course we had no way of knowing any of this.

Our drive back to campus allowed us to re-hash stories of our captures and the marvels of the animals we had observed and handled. We had gotten acquainted with a beautiful piece of the Mojave Desert, and we had met the two most important kangaroo rat species living in the Mojave. I thought this was all just excellent. I knew I wanted more of this.

A few weeks before spring break, that iconic week of annual eccentricity among college students, Dr. Mac placed a notice on the zoology department bulletin board. He was announcing a field trip to Mexico, open to all zoology majors, with promise of a beach where the desert meets the sea in the magical Gulf of California. This was the place John Steinbeck illuminated in his 1951 *The Log from the Sea of Cortez*, which captured his adventures on a six-week springtime cruise around the gulf with his marine biologist friend Ed Ricketts. The realm of the Sea of Cortez contained so much: sea creatures, surrounding Sonoran Desert, Mexico's culture and history, and a hot and dry climate. Signing up for this adventure was, for me, an irresistible leap of joyous expectation. Several of my *Animal Ecology* classmates joined the group that was otherwise made up mostly of junior and senior zoology majors. The professor convened an organizational meeting, with a slide show, to give a flavor of what to expect, how to prepare for the trip, sharing expenses, obtaining the Mexican tourist card, and everything else we needed to know. This looked to me like a dream trip, and it would turn out to be just that.

An arduous day of driving, with regular driver trade-offs, took us more than 700 miles in 13 hours, crossing the mountains again at San Bernardino, heading southwards through the southern Mojave to Palm Desert, then the Salton Sea, and crossing to travel along the Mexican side of the border to Sonoyta, where we headed southward through occasional desert towns and settlements to the big city of Hermosillo, capital of the state of Sonora. The Sonoran Desert, properly prescribed, begins in southeastern California and southwestern Arizona and extends southward, around the northern Gulf of California through the Mexican states of Baja California (on the peninsula) and Sonora (on the continent). Although bright wildflowers dotted the landscape now and then along our way, it was a bleak and spare landscape as we travelled into the state of Sonora along the US border, but this was what I came to embrace. For me, it was a new desert, the Sonoran!

Red, gray, and blackish rocky buttes and volcanic

formations stood out above the sandy desert flats, both at roadside and in the greater expanse of the desert along the border. The sands, variously light tan to reddish and forming massive dune complexes in places, extended from the lower basin of California's Salton Sea region down along the borderlands all the way to the Gulf of California. The biggest and most conspicuous plant in this area is an icon of desert imagery: the saguaro cactus (*Carnegiea gigantea*), the 30 to 40-foot-tall green monsters that rise on heavy trunks to considerable height before extending their upwardly directed arm branches. I had never seen a wild saguaro before, and I was in awe of their grandeur and the variety of their personalities, as conveyed by various, sometimes-odd arrangements of their arms. Despite the urgency of pressing onward in our hot cars with windows rolled down, we had to stop for the saguaros. I wanted to touch a saguaro. We all did. The green flesh on the vertical ridges was smooth and spineless, except for the crests of the ridges, which carried thin, sharp spines, emanating from nodes along each crest. The surfaces in between were touchable. Extending my index finger in between the rows of spines, I rubbed along the plain flesh, feeling the warmth of the massive body of this giant, leafless, green tree that had heated up during the sunny day under a pure blue sky.

Travelling on the main north-south inland route through Sonora, we headed further southward toward the fishing port of Guaymas, considered by some to be the southern limit of the Sonoran Desert, where the landscape transitions to tropical thorn scrub and deciduous forests that extend further south into the state of Sinaloa. Just north of Guaymas we headed westward to the coast and passed through the community of San Carlos, and beyond that on a dirt road to a beach called Los Algodones. At the north end of the beach a point extended outward toward three rocky islands, and we drove onward along a shallow, inland lagoon to the next lonely looking beach to the north, which was backed by a few sections of short rocky bluffs with interdigitating sand dunes. A desert landscape of large shrubs and small thorny trees mixed with cactus stretched out behind the dunes toward hills and rocky buttes further inland. One kind of cactus, tall and rising above the small trees, displayed imposing silhouettes in the dimming skylight. This was the cardón (*Pachycereus pringlei*), slender cousin of the saguaro and typically reaching a similar height. The sheer bulk of a cardón, because of its thinner trunk and branches, appears to be less than that of a saguaro, but the cardón has more extensive branching that arises closer to the ground.

The road seemed to end here at this second beach, and we pulled up and stopped just behind the upper margin of the beach. The sun had set, and we got out of the cars and began moving around in the early twilight to immerse ourselves in the joy of this remote place. Dr. Mac assured us, based on his previous experience, that we could camp comfortably on our own here for the week. Our arrival was initially somewhat boisterous, after the hours of confinement to hot autos streaming across endless desert, but the beauty and solitude of our beach and this desert place provided a sense of awe that quieted us down for the night and continued to sustain our spirits through the week.

We must have had something to eat to extend the snacks and car food that supplied our energy needs over the long day, but after all that time crossing so much territory to reach this new land, we were just glad to be here. Soft, dry sand abounded at the head of the beach, and it was easy to scrape out level spots for our sleeping bags. This would be a quiet night on the sand—with the appearance of stars of unbelievable brightness and clarity. The big dipper has always stood out for me, as originally pointed out to me by my grandfather and father since my earliest childhood, with the two stars of the outer dipper pointing to the north star. "You have to know where north is," they repeated, in a way that I can still hear in my mind. We all settled down eventually and slept in anticipation of a week of fun and exploration at our beach camp.

It doesn't make sense that anyone would have been up particularly early, and with the morning's cool marine air it remained comfortable to stay in the sack, even as the sun rose and signaled a forthcoming day of beautiful beach weather. Many in the group were already indoctrinated with Dr. Mac's formula for cowboy coffee, so the hot water got started on the Coleman stove and soon the smell attracted coffee drinkers to begin the day. To those who showed up in the kitchen area, Dr. Mac directed a few suggestions for setting up folding tables for food preparation and washing dishes, and we more or less organized the boxes of kitchen supplies and iceboxes to form our kitchen. Dr. Mac brought a large chunk of parachute material that we used to form a shade over the kitchen area by stretching the corners with ropes we tied to the surrounding scrubby trees.

Dr. Mac gave us some first-day recommendations and then expounded on what he had already billed as a most worthy activity at this place: fin-and-snorkel diving for lobsters! We had brought along masks, snorkels, and fins, so some of us took an initial morning swim out into the pleasant warm water, also, as it turned out, our main source of bathing for the week. The surf here on our gently sloping beach was minimal, owing to the protection afforded by the Baja California Peninsula that confined the quieter waters of the 700-mile-long Gulf of California against the Mexican mainland. Our position on the continent, near Guaymas, was about half way up, or down if you prefer, the length of the opposing peninsula to our west, far enough away, at 100 miles or so, that we never saw it.

Floating on the surface with masks pointed downward, we stared at rocky reefs in water only ten to fifteen feet deep, representing extensions of the same rock formations that we could see on land, just up from the shore. A pure white floor of sand extended between the occasional rocky reefs, which were narrow, linear formations that seemed to run perpendicular to the shore. Visibility was pretty good here, but the number of fishes was not great. It was pleasant, however, to float on the surface and stare down at colorful fish that poked around the reef, in and out, back and forth with small swells that swept along the rock face.

Some members of our group were previously experienced along the California coast with catching the California spiny lobster, but that was by deep diving with SCUBA gear. Here on our beach, Dr. Mac reported, we were going to get them by free-diving, down along the bases of the little reefs we were exploring on our first morning swim. The lobster here was the same species as in California (*Panulirus interruptus*) and known locally as the langosta roja, or just langosta, as we eventually learned from the locals from nearby villages who passed along the beach occasionally during the week. These lobsters, for some reason not as famous as the "Maine" or Atlantic coast lobsters, don't actually have big pinching claws, but they have plenty of spiny moving tail parts and pointy spines on the carapace of their hard-shelled body to inflict damage to the hands of would-be human predators. Thus the heavy gloves Dr. Mac had advised us to bring for protection. The biggest lobsters were up to about a foot long, and with equally long antennae, and five pairs of legs. We also needed to carry, on our dives, a cloth or net bag of some kind, into which our booty could be stuffed upon each successful grab of a lobster out of its hidey hole in the reef rock. These lobsters are nocturnal, and when we found them in the day they were resting, lodged back in crevasses or under ledges in the reef. The prized edible part of the lobster, as with shrimp, is the tail, and the tail of these lobsters is a massive muscle that propels the animal backwards, with a pulsing flexion, through the water. The tail makes up about half of the body length and is a couple of inches thick.

Diving for lobsters became a daily pastime on our beach. The harvest was held in the shade until time for cooking—another ritual we learned from Dr. Mac, who brought along an enormous beat-up metal pot, blackened from campfire smoke, just for this purpose. Gathering scraps of firewood from the upland scrub, we built a fire on the beach in the early evening, boiled seawater in the pot placed right into the fire, and, as per the traditional fate of so many different crustacean species (from prawns and crayfish to crabs and lobsters) we dropped our hapless prey into boiling water for a short cooking process that turned them bright orange and rendered them ready for consumption. Tearing the hot tail off the rest of the body yielded the consumable prize, which we accompanied with nothing more than some melted butter and freshly squeezed lemon juice. Delicious!

We seemed to survive well on a diet of beans, boiled in pots and prepared in the Mexican fashion, as well as tomatoes, onions, and avocados, with liberal sharing of various bottles of hot sauce. We obtained excellent local tortillas from a tortillería in town, and we gradually supplement our initial imported food supplies with local groceries from Guaymas. Our ice boxes remained cold with more ice from town, and of course plenty of bottled beer from the local distributor. It also seemed necessary to sample, in varying quantities, the close-to-cheapest tequila that could be obtained from the local outlet, urging it down with sucks on lemon wedges and licks of salt shaken onto the little pocket on the back of the hand between thumb and forefinger. This ritual was shared, by senior members of the group, as the approved way to consume the wretched distillate directly from the bottle.

The prevailing spirit of the week was to enjoy the remarkable beach setting and take it easy. Our entire existence, other than occasional runs into town for supplies, was right here at our camp. Social bonds developed with all the time we had, free of studies, to relax, swim, sun ourselves, and rest in the shade. We walked up and down the beach and took short hikes up to a higher rocky bluff behind the open desert scrublands. From our camp we could see a native palm oasis up a tiny canyon that indented the bluff. We hiked up there to enjoy a fresh-water shower from a small, trickling waterfall that descended out of a spring in the rocks above. This local spot of water was a surprise, and from up there we looked back down on the dry scrub and beach below.

The week could not pass without opportunities to meet a few local desert critters. A common lizard that seemed to erupt out of the dunes and associated bushes when we walked in among them was the zebra-tailed lizard (*Callisaurus draconoides*). This small and slender reptile, mottled gray and brown on the back, but white underneath, was well deserving of the zebra-tail name, because that's what you saw when they ran away from you. The bottom of the tail was bent upwards in a curve to reveal a set of alternating black bars against a white base as the animal streaked away from you at high speed on its two hind feet, with the upper body elevated off the ground. This pattern of locomotion is a reptilian variation on the bipedal theme of kangaroo rats, who hop simultaneously on both feet at the same instant; these lizards, in contrast, are alternating strokes of their left and right legs as they sprint across the sand.

Crowded somehow into the zoology department Landrover that Dr. Mac drove down to Mexico was a box of the usual rodent traps, just not as many as we had taken on our class field trips. On several evenings we set out the traps, and I was excited to get out and check them to see what we would find. I was amazed to discover that the local kangaroo rat species here was the same Merriam's kangaroo rat that we met in the Mojave Desert. The population here was near to the southernmost geographic limit of the species, a short distance south of us in northern Sinaloa State. It was a good thing, I thought, to know that a single species could develop a survival formula that allowed it to become successful over such a broad geographic range that extended from the Mojave and through the entire Sonoran Desert. My favorite big kangaroo rat, the desert kangaroo rat from the Mojave, also has a big geographic range, but just not quite as big as Merriam's. It turns out that the desert kangaroo rat extends southward to a point only about 100 miles north of where we were located near Guaymas.

Where kangaroo rats live, one pretty much always finds pocket mice, and indeed we found a rather large pocket mouse, Bailey's pocket mouse (now known as *Chaetodipus baileyi*), in our traps here as well. The success of this pocket mouse maps out very closely to the geographic bounds of the Sonoran Desert, making it an exclusive member of the Sonoran Desert fauna. As I was also coming to recognize, a good desert in North America also needs a woodrat, and we found signs of cactus nibbling and house building, as well as trapping success, with a local species, the white-throated woodrat (*Neotoma albigula*). This species is well known across the Mexican continental part of the Sonoran Desert and eastward into the fourth great American desert, the Chihuahuan Desert.

As with any group of college students approaching the end of a magical week of spring vacation, we had sad feelings as we completed the last day on our beach. We had to return to campus, alas, to finish the semester. The drive home was long and tiring, and it brought us back to reality.

As the detailed memories of our week in the Sonoran Desert where it meets the Gulf of California began to fade, I became aware of the more enduring memories of neighboring Mexico and its landscape and seascape. I didn't understand then all the subtle differences among North America's great deserts, but I had obtained an initial look at the deeper reaches of the Sonoran Desert. The saguaros and the cardóns, the rocks and sands, kangaroo rats and pocket mice, lizards—they were all part of the beauty. For indescribable reasons, the anchor to my impression of the entire biota and the landscape was my personal discovery that Merriam's kangaroo rat, a species shared with the Mojave Desert, was living here at the southern extreme of its geographic range and of the Sonoran Desert. Dr. Mac had shown me yet more, and I was able to add these initial impressions to the experiences in my lifetime memory bank.

One of my responses to the adventures of my sophomore-year springtime was to acquire a rather plain pair of high-top, lace-up leather boots at the local Sears store. As I broke them in, I began to feel the boots were becoming part of my identity with the desert, and I also knew they would protect my ankles from the legendary strike of a rattlesnake. I would eventually wear out two more pairs of these boots over the next seven years before completing my PhD.

What more in the way of deserts could Dr. Mac show us in late May, with only a couple of weeks remaining in the semester? I was ready for the last field trip, boots and all, and Dr. Mac announced that we were going northward beyond the Mojave into yet another of North America's deserts: the Great Basin, and the state of Nevada. Over a lengthy seven-hour drive we witnessed the transition out of the Mojave heading northward along the eastern side of the Sierra Nevada. We passed the last, northernmost creosote bushes and entered the Owens Valley.

To reach Nevada we took off eastward across the Owens Valley, near the small town of Big Pine, and climbed into the White and Inyo Mountains, which we crossed on a narrow two-lane paved road where these two mountain blocks meet, at 7,313-foot Westgard Pass. These mountains are just the beginning of an entire series of north-south ranges separated by intervening internally draining valleys with sagebrush and salt-flat bottoms that make up the Great Basin Desert, extending eastward to Utah and northward to southern Idaho and Oregon. We dropped down from the White-Inyo Range into the southern end of twenty-five-mile-long Fish Lake Valley, drab, scrubby lowlands, with occasional range cattle standing among the shrubs and sometimes wandering out across the road. Five miles after crossing the Nevada border we passed the small settlement of Dyer and continued northward.

Of the various alluvial fans flanking the valley and the salt flats and sand-dune formations in the valley bottom, we were going to seek out the dunes in particular. That was where we should find our target for this trip: a special community of rodents of the family Heteromyidae at the western edge of the Great Basin. The theme of kangaroo rats and pocket mice would continue here in a new way that Dr. Mac wanted to show us. As we drove along, we began to see impressive sand dunes rising up from the valley floor. Greasewood (*Sarcobatus*), saltbush (*Atriplex*), and other bushes stabilized the dunes, which were shaped into sandy pockets and rising banks of sand, ten or fifteen feet high in places. We learned that the sands were derived from old lakebeds, now dry, that last held major bodies of water less than ten thousand years ago as the last glacial period came to an end.

Arriving in late afternoon, we prepared to set traps first. We could find our camping place afterwards, using a dirt side-road that led up an alluvial fan. We pulled off onto the shoulder of the highway next to a promising set of dunes to string out the traps in the usual way. Walking through the soft, loose sand made for a pleasant feeling in my feet. As I reached the crest of each dune, my steps produced small avalanches that gave way beneath my new leather boots. The air was dry and cool, with temperatures that reflected our high elevation, about 5,000 feet, even in the bottom of the valley. The mountains to our east rose to nearly 10,000 feet and those to the west even higher, with snow showing on the highest peaks.

Dr. Mac knew this place from earlier research he had done here, and he did not want to wait for trap results the next morning to surprise us. He made it clear why he had brought us to the Fish Lake Valley dunes. We were going to meet a new kind of heteromyid rodent that was neither kangaroo rat nor pocket mouse, and that was the pallid kangaroo mouse (with the big Latin mouthful: *Microdipodops pallidus*). The "micro" part of the name suggested small size, and that meant smaller than a kangaroo rat. This species and only one other in the same genus are the world's only two species of kangaroo mice, and they are found only in the Great Basin, centered in the state of Nevada. These little kangaroo mice are basically a small version of the kangaroo rats, but bigger than the pocket mice and otherwise sharing many of the common characteristics of the family: seeds as a dietary staple, physiological adaptations for survival without water in arid habitats, and a body design of big head, big feet, and long tail associated with bipedal locomotion. The pallid kangaroo mouse is strongly associated with sand dunes and rather rare across its small geographic range, which is also the case with the closely related dark kangaroo mouse (*Microdipodops megacephalus*). The pallid kangaroo mouse occurs in the more southerly portion of the Great Basin and the dark kangaroo mouse more to the north. Because kangaroo mice resemble kangaroo rats more than pocket mice, it makes sense that the evolutionary lineage of kangaroo mice, within their family, is more closely connected to kangaroo rats than pocket mice.

After another happy evening of food, music, and some campfire nonsense in our isolated campsite at the base of the mountains to the west, we eventually had a good night's rest beneath the starry sky. Next morning we fired ourselves up with the usual coffee and breakfast and drove back down to our trap lines on the dunes. The core of the rodent community in the Fish Lake Valley dune system turned out to be a heteromyid quartet: two species of kangaroo rats, one species of pocket mouse, and the celebrated new kid on the block—the pallid kangaroo mouse. It was clear on first inspection that the kangaroo mouse, with its soft fur, sandy coloration, and diminutive stature was perhaps a notch up on cuteness over the bigger kangaroo rats. The unbelievable appearance of the kangaroo mouse is due to further exaggeration of the disproportionate features of the kangaroo rat body plan. The kangaroo mouse is basically half head and half torso, or as some have said: half head and half butt. As a result, the ears fan out above the torso midway along the body, and as on a kangaroo rat, the eyes are big and dark colored. The feet are also long — making, once again, an excellent hopping machine. Some of us wanted to cuddle the kangaroo mice in our hands, making a light cup around the animal, as it wiggled its feet, pressing with the hind feet and just tickling and digging with the tiny front feet, or hands as we like to call them.

The kangaroo rats in the quartet were both species we'd already met elsewhere, providing another lesson in biogeography and biodiversity. They were the same two we found at Piute Butte in the Mojave Desert: Merriam's kangaroo rat and the desert kangaroo rat. But now, within the Great Basin these two were known marginally only from the western parts of Nevada adjacent to California. We also recalled that Merriam's kangaroo rat had shown itself to us at the southern extreme of its range at the bottom of the Sonoran Desert on our spring-break trip to Mexico. The pocket mouse we caught in Fish Lake Valley, the little pocket mouse (*Perognathus longimembris*), lived up to its "little" name at the size of what I think of as a large peanut, barely weighing a quarter of an ounce and making it North America's smallest rodent. This is a species I later investigated in the Owen Valley as part of my dissertation research.

Since the earliest days of their discovery, the kangaroo mice — restricted only to the Great Basin Desert — have been adulated and endeared for their delicate structure and unusual body proportions, for their quaintness and rarity, and for the economy of their spare lives in an obscure and demanding environment. They were first discovered by modern science in the fall of 1890 by the great mammalogist Vernon Bailey (1864-1942), who practiced his career as Chief

Field Naturalist with the US Bureau of Biological Survey. In a stirring tribute to kangaroo mice in his 1936 monograph *The Mammals and Life Zones of Oregon* (where the northern species is also found), Bailey wrote:

> "With all our intelligence and versatility of adaptation we are still far behind such animals in the perfection of physical mechanism for our needs, and we can surely learn humility if not wisdom from many of our inferior mammalian brothers."

We had a long day ahead of us to return to the Los Angeles area. We were exhausted from both the field trip and from the entirety of our responsibilities at the college as the semester drew to a close. Dr. Mac had given us more experience on yet another field trip, with new samplings of nature, of the Great Basin, and of an unlikely creature—the kangaroo mouse. I felt a great sense of delight and satisfaction, even if I was tired.

Shortly after our last field trip the semester was over, and I knew I had experienced adventures that would somehow direct my life. I still revere the field trips of *Zoology 157* as the supreme highlight of the course because it was there, out in nature, where all the academic principles and theory came to life. In fact, that's where they first became believable and understandable to me. Back on campus Dr. Mac, in well- organized fashion, introduced us in the lecture hall to many dimensions of ecology. In the weeks without field trips we also met in a lab to study museum specimens of the mammals, birds, reptiles, and amphibians of southern California's deserts in order to become able to identify them and give their common and scientific names, along with their geographic distributions and basic natural history features.

Dr. Mac's lectures, which presented reports on recently published research, provided a broad view of ecology. He also showed us his own enthusiasm for the physiological and behavioral adaptations of animals to desert environments. He once expanded on the theme of the evolutionary success of kangaroo rats and pocket mice in North American deserts by telling us about rodents that inhabit the deserts of Earth's other continents. Desert rodents, by their sheer numbers in all these desert ecosystems, play major roles as consumers of seeds and other plant materials, as dispersers of seeds and spores, and as prey for many predators. Rodents that belong to other family lineages living on other continents have evolved the same anatomical and physiological specializations as our North American kangaroo rats, kangaroo mice, and pocket mice (family Heteromyidae). These patterns, by which similar features have evolved elsewhere in other lineages and in response to the same environmental selective pressures, represent an evolutionary phenomenon known as parallel evolution or convergent evolution. The phenomenon has been given those names because the process has happened independently, in parallel, and converging on the same sets of adaptations. I was amazed that the marvels I discovered in the heteromyid rodents of North America's deserts have arisen several other times in other rodent lineages that evolved in deserts elsewhere on Earth!

For special reading Dr. Mac selected a 1964 book by Knut Schmidt-Nielsen entitled *Desert Animals-Physiological Problems of Heat and Water*. I still keep that book in my personal library as a memory of my experience with Dr. Mac. It has chapters on kangaroo rats and how they get along without drinking water or eating succulent food because of the powerful water-reclaiming capacity of their kidneys; and on woodrats and how they eat cactus throughout the year as a source of water and how they avoid desert heat by living in insulated houses they construct out of sticks, stones, and cactus; and on lizards such as desert iguanas and how they behaviorally control their body temperature by selecting appropriate times and places to be active.

The meaning I found in Dr. Mac's field trips certainly came from spending time in nature. But of course there was more. The warmth and caring attributes of Dr. Mac's serious personality and his dedication to teaching reinforced the experiences and positive memories that my fellow student comrades and I obtained. Dr. Mac provided a leadership role by allowing us to develop our own first-hand appreciation of places and of the creatures who lived there. Any resulting intellectual synthesis was happily, in my opinion, derived because the whole process of engagement with science began outdoors, in nature.

Three great American Deserts—the Mojave, the Sonoran, and the Great Basin—each showed me their character, their beauty, and their biological diversity on these visits early in my life. I wanted to share and I wanted to return to these places, not only the broad expanse of each desert, but the particular places I first visited. I returned later with my parents and youngest brother to Piute Butte to show off kangaroo rats, and I returned as a graduate student to share the same place and the kangaroo rats again with new students at the university. I returned to the same Mexican beach north of Guaymas with more student friends over each of the following two spring breaks. I returned to Nevada's Fish Lake Valley as a young professor, bringing along my first PhD student, who ended up conducting research on how the kangaroo rats, kangaroo mice, and pocket mice selected seeds of different sizes for their diets. It seems that remembering places and returning to them expands on the original meaning they hold for us.

Of all the living wonder we met, I somehow was most fondly delighted by kangaroo rats. It was their soft fur and sandy colorations, big head and bulging cheek pouches, large and powerful hind feet, and the long tail with its terminal fringe. The story of kangaroo rats surviving on limited and unpredictable resources and under extreme physical conditions, and the story of the evolutionary success of so many species of them in western North America's deserts—these were signs to me of an extraordinary creature.

I also can't forget the small patch of Los Angeles Basin semidesert, just a few miles away from my college, where I met my first kangaroo rat. The natural habitat I saw on that first *Animal Ecology* field trip still lies there much as it did in 1965, with the full complement of pungent coastal sage scrub and chaparral. Remarkably, it has been protected from development because it lies on land administered by a water conservation agency, and the alluvial fan remains a dangerous zone of potential flooding that makes it unsuitable for building. That place is, in my mind, a good piece of desert and a place of beauty, a deep memory.

In 2017 I found an opportunity to return there on the occasion of the fiftieth reunion of my college graduation. I invited a fellow *Animal Ecology* classmate to return there with me on an April morning. We walked together across the same sand and gravel and among the same shrubs, breathing the warm, dry air filled with smells of sage and chaparral. In patches of sand we saw tracks of kangaroo rats and nearby holes leading into their burrows.

As we prepared to leave, I bent down to the gravelly surface and picked up two small cobbles of granite, white and heavily peppered with black spots. I held them, one in each hand, and realized they represented a connection to this place, and I took them along with me. I kept one, now on my desk.

A month later I took the other stone along with me on a visit to my dear and now elderly professor friend, Dr. Mac. We shared more memories of our times together in the field. I gave him the rock, and he told me he was pleased.

9

UNDERGROUND MYSTERIES
OF KANGAROO RATS

My head was extending downward, suspended below the cold surface of the winter desert into a hole I had shoveled out during the previous several hours. I braced myself on my elbows against the warm and humid sand walls of the cavity, my legs reaching upward to the surface. I held a small microphone in one hand, while fingers of the other hand traced the route of a carefully maintained passageway within the burrow system of a kangaroo rat. I had dug a deep hole to the side of the descending rodent tunnels in order to form a vertical face of sand. This deeper hole allowed me to excavate the tunnels carefully, without collapsing them, which would have happened if I were simply digging downward on top of them. Instead, I shaved the sand off the large, vertical face with a small hand trowel in order to follow the course of each individual tunnel. I peered now into a dark tunnel, just a couple of inches in diameter. I snapped on the switch of a flashlight to let my eyes take in the smooth, sandy walls and slightly flattened floor of the previously dark tunnel that disappeared further downward beyond my excavation. Nobody else but kangaroo rats had ever been down here. I had definitely entered somebody else's space, and I was expecting shortly to come upon the animal's winter nest.

It was a cold, late December day in 1970, out in the shadscale scrub of California's Owens Valley, east of the Sierra Nevada. This arid valley reaches northward from the Mojave Desert and forms a transitional link into the Great Basin Desert. My excavation was the fulfillment of a curiosity I had developed over the previous five years since I had first met kangaroo rats. Looking at the in-and-out holes on top of kangaroo rat mounds had made me want to know where the holes led. I wanted to see first-hand the architecture of the burrow systems and discover anything possible about the behavior of kangaroo rats. I was now a graduate student in the fourth year of pursuing my PhD in ecology.

I spoke into the microphone, attached to a battery-operated spool-to-spool magnetic tape recorder, producing a spontaneous and rather awkward narrative that I later typed up:

> "...It's now 1:45 in the afternoon and we've just arrived at the location of *Dipodomys microps* 266, 45 gram female, run 49. She's right underneath the red spot where she's been every time I've measured the last several days.
>
> I've come across several tunnels as I've come right near where the nest is, and these tunnels

are 4 to 5 centimeters wide and about that high, and they're in moist soil. Checking with the probe, we think she's in the nest. I can see a small hole in there that's about 2 centimeters diameter, which is in the grassy nest material and the actual entrance to the nest.

Okay, now just up above the nesting chamber—I haven't gone into it yet—I found a sort of bathroom chamber again, which is about 15 centimeters away and 10 centimeters higher towards the surface, and it's in a moist area, and has that strong smell again, and this chamber is about 9 centimeters high and 18 to 20 centimeters average in diameter. The chamber I just described had just a few bits of plant material, nothing very substantial, and quite a number of scats. Mostly just sort of smelly dirt...."

Deciphering the meaning of this recorded text requires some background as to how I became ready to dig up a burrow, and how I actually knew that it was the home of a particular individual of a particular species.

Digging up the underground burrow system of a kangaroo rat amounted to a necessary exploration as far as I was concerned. How else could I fully understand the behavior of the animals without seeing, touching, smelling, and mapping out the space in which they spend most of their lives? Of the questions I outlined for my research proposal, several could only be answered by directly exploring the underground dwellings.

My plan was to make comparisons, looking for differences among species in how they conduct their lives. Different life styles should minimize competition between species. Did the shrub hillocks under which the rodents dug their burrows differ in some way? How deep were the burrows? Could I figure out where the animals spend their time? My overall study was a comprehensive comparison among the three most abundant rodent species in the community: the chisel-toothed or Great Basin kangaroo rat (*Dipodomys microps*), Merriam's kangaroo rat (*Dipodomys merriami*), and the little pocket mouse (*Perognathus longimembris*), all of which belong to the rodent family called the Heteromyidae.

I made the excavation that I narrated into the tape recorder after I had already spent a year and a half on my project. I had to establish ahead of time which individual belonged in any particular burrow system, as well as some history of its occupation of the space. That way I could better interpret what I found in the tunnels and cavities down below.

I wanted to know how kangaroo rats respond to seasonal changes in the environment, for example, changes in temperature that would produce changes in their rate of energy expenditure — their metabolism. To accomplish this I needed to document temperatures in various microenvironments of my study area — in the air, on the surface, and in the soil. I used a wind-up clock apparatus with circular 24-hour graph paper to record air temperature on the surface at animal height. I got ahold of some tiny sensors (temperature sensitive resistors fixed on the end of wires) that I plugged into a portable battery-operated box with a temperature gauge. I used these sensors each time I worked on my study area to record temperature with probes

I placed in the air at various heights above the ground and in the soil at various depths below the surface. I also obtained general weather data from a US Weather Bureau station about 15 miles north of my study area.

I monitored the rodent populations by monthly live-trapping and environmental measurements to get a picture of seasonality over three winters and the subsequent breeding seasons. Reproduction by rodent populations in the Mojave Desert and Owens Valley coincides strategically with the pulse of new green annual and perennial vegetation that begins to grow with winter rains and allows mother rodents to get their young weaned and out on their own before the summer drought. The drought usually begins by May, with little or no rain for the following six months or so.

January and February generally had the coldest air temperatures, and July and August the warmest. I had wondered if kangaroo rats and pocket mice both hibernated, and that question was answered by my monthly live-trapping surveys. The kangaroo rats showed up in good numbers in every month of the year, with nighttime air temperatures as warm as 86°F in summer or as cold as minus 2°F in winter. The little pocket mice, on the other hand, disappeared from the trapping records through the autumn and winter, in hibernation, amounting to an absence of up to six months while they turned down their metabolism and body temperature to the lowest possible levels that matched the temperature of the surrounding soil.

The underground existence of nocturnally active desert rodents is not just a matter of where they spend the daytime, but where they spend most of their entire lives, protected by the security of their underground passageways and in total or near-total darkness. I mention "most of their lives underground" because even at night they emerge only at intervals onto the surface to forage, and thus they are spending much of the night in their burrows as well.

The five-foot-deep soil-temperature probe that I installed on my grid gave me an important record of annual temperature cycles in the soil, and those were very similar each year. I obtained these measurements each time I visited the area by connecting the wires and plugs (emerging from the top of the probe) to an electronic box with a temperature gauge. I was really pleased when I finally managed to get the probe secured into the ground, and considering all the effort it required, I left the probe in the ground permanently. I had made an eight-foot-long soil auger (a drill for dirt) in the zoology shop and used it to bore out the hole for the probe. In addition to the five-foot probe, I constructed a smaller, portable probe that I could easily force into the loose soil near the surface to a depth of 16 inches, after first driving in and then removing a slightly larger rod to prepare a guide hole. I used the small, portable probe to make a lot of measurements of soil temperature in the shallow soil above rodent burrows. I made both the probes out of hollow fiberglass fishing-rod stock, so that I could glue the sensors into the wall and thread the wires upward through the hollow inside to the top. The deep probe's sensors measured temperature at 50, 100, and 150 centimeters, which is equivalent to 20 inches, 39 inches, and 59 inches. The shallow probe measured at 4, 8, 12, and 16 inches depth.

The story of deep soil temperatures is a cycle between two annual extremes. The warmest temperatures at 20 inches were achieved in early August during prolonged summer heat, but deeper down at 5 feet the summer peak did not occur until late August or September, because it took more time for the heat to flow downward to cool the deeper soil. The summer maximum was 80°F at 20 inches, but only 72°F at five feet, which says that a deeper burrow is a cooler burrow in summer.

Recording the cycling of soil temperature through the year showed me that the shallow versus deep extremes were reversed about every six months. In other words, in the coldest part of winter the soil was warmer the deeper you went. The annual minimum of 50°F at 5 feet was achieved in February or early March, but in any event the most thermally efficient place to hang out in winter was as deep as you could go. That corresponds exactly with the rule for summer efficiency, namely, the deeper the better. An amusing feature of this twice-yearly flip-flop of the soil temperature gradient was that between the two extremes there were two periods when the vertical temperature profile was essentially uniform from shallow to deep, and coincidentally those situations prevailed very close to the March and September equinoxes. That means that animals underground at those times could spend their time at any depth, with no consequences for their comfort and energy efficiency, because of the vertical uniformity of temperature.

Figuring out how to know for certain where kangaroo rats lived and didn't live, and which rat lived in which burrow, was no easy matter in the late 1960s. The radio-transmitting equipment and satellite-tracking devices that are attached to small animals so commonly in wildlife studies in the new millennium were not available when I was a graduate student. But one day a fellow graduate student office mate introduced me to his brother-in-law, who was an assistant professor of nuclear engineering at the university. That introduction was the beginning of how I became able to unlock some secrets of where desert rodents go and how deep when they disappear into their burrows.

Craig was just the man I needed to meet, and at just the right time. The young nuclear energy professor was himself energetic—and fun loving. He was heavily occupied with his research concerning the earthquake safety of nuclear power plants, but somehow he found time to assist by opening the door to technology that helped me satisfy my curiosity about the underground lives of desert rodents. Perhaps Craig took a liking to me and my rodents because we offered him an amusing divergence from the classroom and we catered to his love of the desert. Desert rodents had no particular economic or political significance, nor had any specific conservation issues been raised at the time. For me the attraction was the joy of getting to know mysterious little creatures in a remote and obscure environment and the fact that nothing more was at stake than pure nature. I sensed that Craig liked that too.

Craig welcomed me enthusiastically to the nuclear energy lab and introduced me to the graduate students, technicians, and professors. They were all working on projects that used the university's research reactor to produce radioactive materials. Their projects ranged from analyzing the first rocks that had just been brought back from the moon to producing radioisotopes that could be used to detect and treat cancer. Craig was aware that a few ecologists had placed radioactive tags on animals in order to track them with portable Geiger counters, so we started with a literature search and found nearly 20 published papers reporting how ecologists had located and tracked animals in their natural habitat. Soon we were discussing how we could do even more than this with kangaroo rats and pocket mice. Craig thought we could use measurements of the intensity of the emitted radiation at the surface to determine how deep the animals were resting down in the soil.

I was surprised to learn how neutrons could be used to bombard various materials to make them radioactive, and how the resulting alpha, beta, and gamma radiation varied with regard to the distance and intensity with which it traveled through other materials, such as soil, after it was emitted from a radioactive source. What I learned was not entirely casual, as I was required to take a course in radiation theory and safety. That qualified me to work around the reactor and to travel on public roads with irradiated material in a vehicle, under a special permit, so that I could take "hot" material out into the desert for tagging rodents. I had to wear a radiation safety badge that, similarly to photographic film, became irradiated by any radioactive sources to which I was exposed. When I turned the badge in to the radiation safety officer, he evaluated the amount of exposure I had received in any week or month. My protocols were all designed to minimize exposure and remain safe. In the end I became confident through all our calculations and monitoring that neither the rodents nor I would experience any threats to our health.

We figured out that the element gold, of all precious things, would be the best for our application. We could slip a thin, short length (one centimeter long) of pure gold wire just beneath the skin on the back of a kangaroo rat or pocket mouse, and that would be our tag. Gold was a strong gamma-radiation emitter. The tiny and compact 40-milligram wire would be sufficient to produce the signal we required. Gamma radiation had the advantage over alpha and beta (emitted by other isotopes) of maintaining greater intensity over greater distance through the soil. The half-life of an isotope describes the amount of time over which a radiated source will decay to 50% of its original intensity, and the half-life of gold is only 2.7 days. This meant that the radiation would only be useful for about a week, and in fact that by three weeks from the date of irradiation in the reactor, the gamma-emitting gold would have decreased to a level of no remaining detectable radioactivity. Our subsequent recovery and ongoing observation for many months of 60 animals after they carried the radioactive tags revealed no apparent damaging effects to normal appearance and function. Once Craig and I worked out the basic procedures for preparing and installing the gold tags on the animals, I was able to capitalize on that by finding the home burrow of each animal.

I tagged the animals in the early evening by setting out traps at dusk, checking the traps a couple of hours later, removing an animal from its trap, and gently inserting the gold wire through a tiny skin puncture on the back, near the shoulders. I immediately released each animal to resume its normal evening activity. I did all of this tagging in a nearby area that was separate from my usual long-term monitoring grids where I was trapping and releasing animals that I did not want to disturb, either with the isotope tagging or with the excavation of burrow systems. I also made sure that the trapping locations of the individual animals I tagged were far enough apart that I could be certain, once I found the burrow locations of tagged animals, which animal was which. To be absolutely sure, I also later re-trapped each tagged animal to reconfirm the proximity of its trapping locations to its home burrow that was emitting the radioactive signal.

On the morning after tagging I set out immediately with my Geiger counter to find where each tagged animal was holed up in its burrow. Although the counter box had a needle gauge showing radiation intensity, the cue for me was the audible crackling produced when I approached a radioactive source, which I picked up by wearing headphones plugged into the counter. For convenience while wandering around in the daytime searching for a kangaroo rat or pocket mouse in its burrow, I modified the expensive piece of lab equipment by duct-taping a bamboo cane to the Geiger tube at the end of the cable extending from the small instrument box, which I supported over my shoulder with a strap. That way I could walk around comfortably, waving the tube over the ground, probing into the base of bushes on top of the hillocks and other possible burrow locations until I started detecting a buzz. Moving back and forth to compare stronger and weaker signals, I eventually zeroed in on top of the hot spot that gave the strongest buzz. That was where the animal was ensconced in its burrow. Located! I placed a colored flag in the closest bush, usually right on top of the soil mound that contained the burrow. All the field work associated with each tagged animal had to be done within a few days, or up to a week in some cases, of the initial tagging, because the clock was ticking on the decay of gold's radioactivity to an undetectable level. Once each animal was located, it was time to start making observations on the animal's behavior and the characteristics of its burrow site.

Although I enjoyed the solitude and apparent privacy of working in the quietness of a remote desert place where nobody else came around to inquire or interfere with my activities, I did learn, a few months into my daytime surveys with the Geiger counter—ear phones on my head and bamboo stick waving around over the ground—that I attracted some local attention. Back in the nearby town among county road crew members who drove by my study area on their way to maintain gravel roads in the remote desert mountains and valleys of eastern Inyo County, a rumor had surfaced that someone from the university (identified by the official markings on my vehicle) was exploring the Owens Valley for uranium. I was amused that the technology I was using to explore desert rodents had produced such a sophisticated impression.

One of the first things I began to explore about each tagged animal, once I had located its burrow, was how deep it was staying down in its burrow and at what temperature. For several days in a row I returned repeatedly during the daytime to each burrow. Slowly and gently I stepped up to the burrow site with my Geiger-counter tube lowered to the surface and sweeping around to find the spot that gave the most intense reading, listening through my earphones as the buzzing intensified. I recorded the time and intensity of the Geiger-counter reading on my clipboard and then spray-painted a small red dot on the sand where I had obtained the hottest signal. Using my system for acquiring soil temperatures, I would be able to project the temperature where the animal was resting after calculating the depth based on the Geiger counter's reading.

During the first tests that Craig and I made of our

methods, we had buried gold wires at various depths in the soil and then measured the radiation intensity at each depth, recording also the time of the measurement, which we had to relate to the passage of time since initial irradiation of the gold in the reactor. With this information and further computations we could estimate the depth of a radioactive tag on an animal. So, as I proceeded with the repeated behavioral observations of the locations of tagged animals, I was able to compute the range of depths and temperatures at which each animal was resting over the course of several days.

I made the first observations of location, depth, and soil temperature of kangaroo rats and pocket mice in the spring and summer of 1970, and I found the animals were moving around within their burrows during the day, typically reappearing at several different preferred positions. I also found by late spring and summer that some individual kangaroo rats and pocket mice were relocating from day to day to each of two or three different nearby burrows. In the winter of 1970–71 (December and January) I found each individual kangaroo rat only at a single spot and within the same, single burrow system, which I subsequently confirmed was because they had constructed a winter nest and were exclusively spending their daytime resting hours in that one spot, the nest.

For each of my depth observations of an animal resting in its burrow, I estimated the soil temperature surrounding the animal using either of two sources of temperature data. When the depth was 20 inches or greater I simply used the current reading for that date that I got from the deep permanently buried temperature probe. When the depth was less than 20 inches, I used the small thin probe containing four sensors at 4, 8, 12, and 16 inches to measure the temperatures at the immediate time of my observation by inserting the probe at a point close to the red spot I had painted atop the burrow. By reviewing all my accumulating soil temperature data, I learned that the temperature at 16 inches or deeper would never vary during any 24-hour period by more than one degree Celsius. This means that I only needed to make multiple site-specific measurements of temperature for animals that were inhabiting the top 16 inches of the soil. The temperature at deeper locations was stable (within one degree), but the temperature in shallower soils would cycle significantly during the day, from the highest in late afternoon to the lowest in early morning, at the end of nighttime.

Altogether I studied 60 rodents in their burrows for several days at a time over the course of the seasons, consisting of 25 chisel-toothed kangaroo rats, 15 Merriam's kangaroo rats, and 20 little pocket mice. From largest to smallest, the body weight of these species ranged from about 2 ounces (the weight of ten 25-cent pieces) for chisel tooth, to an ounce and a fourth (six 25-cent pieces) for Merriam's to a mere fourth of an ounce (three pennies) for little pocket mouse, a precious tiny creature who is, in fact, the smallest of all North American rodents.

I found an interesting ecological separation among these three species, as to how they segregated themselves into burrow systems located in hillocks of different sizes. By measuring each soil mound and the bush on top of it for each individual I studied, I found that bigger rodents occupied bigger mounds with bigger bushes. Specifically, on average, chisel tooth burrow hillocks were 26 inches in height and had 33-inch-tall bushes on them, whereas Merriam's mounds were only 16 inches high with 22-inch bushes, and the modest mounds of little pocket mice averaged only 13 inches in height and held small shrubs only 17 inches tall. This seems to reflect one of nature's ways, the sharing of resources among species based on their body size.

I made most of my observations of depths and temperatures where the animals were locating themselves before I excavated any burrows to measure the actual dimensions and locations of tunnels and resting chambers.

The areas close to the surface where animals rested (resting chambers) were for each species about two to three times the diameter of the typical tunnels that led all around within their burrow systems. Typical tunnel diameters corresponded with the differences in body size of the three species, with little pocket mouse tunnels only about three quarters of an inch in diameter, Merriam's kangaroo rat tunnels about two inches, and chisel-toothed kangaroo rat tunnels two and a half to three inches in diameter. The closest tunnels to the surface were those of the little pocket mouse, with barely half an inch of soil serving as the roof of the tunnel. Clearly the structural integrity of the tiny tunnels of these little mice was guaranteed because of the small size of the mouse and its tunnels, whereas kangaroo rats would be unable to maintain stable tunnels that close to the surface. As I discovered, this allowed for some more versatile fine tuning of behavior on the part of pocket mice with regard to the variety of temperatures available at various times of day in the upper soil layers.

The general depths of resting locations and associated soil temperatures were similar in all three species in the summer. They were nearly all resting most of the time at temperatures in the range of 78 to 86°F. The reason this is an efficient comfort zone for these rodents is that it's just below temperatures that would cause heat stress, forcing increased body water loss, and it's above the colder temperatures (deep in the ground) that would require them to produce extra metabolic heat in order to maintain the warmth of their normal body temperature. In early summer the rodents all achieved the soil temperature comfort zone of 78 to 86°F at depths of about eight inches. Closer to the surface was too hot! And by later in the summer, in August, as the entire soil column was heating up seasonally, the rodents were resting deeper down, at about 12 inches depth. As I pointed out earlier, most of the animals moved around during the day within their burrow systems to various alternative spots. As I measured temperatures in those spots,

I found that they were shifting to spots with more favorable temperatures, for example, from a spot below sunny soil surface in the morning to a spot beneath shaded soil in the afternoon.

Switching among nearby burrows from day to day and moving around within a burrow during the day pretty much stopped once the kangaroo rats built their nests in autumn, which meant that in the late fall and winter I was consistently finding them in that same location each day. And with colder temperatures near the surface in autumn, the kangaroo rats and their nests were deeper down in the soil than they'd been in summer. The bigger chisel-toothed kangaroo rats built their nests at about 16 inches depth, whereas the Merriam's kangaroo rats, more delicate and sensitive to cold temperature because of their smaller size, showed a tendency for much deeper nests, on average about three feet, but as deep as five. In fact that's why I had difficulty finding Merriam's kangaroo rats in their nests using the radioactive signals of the gold wire tags, and I completely failed to find eight of the Merriam's that I tagged in the winter studies. Apparently they were so deep as to be out of range for detection of the radioactive signal. I obtained no observations of pocket mouse winter nests, because they were hibernating and thus unavailable for me to capture them on the surface at night in the first place.

The advantage of a nest for a small rodent in the cool winter soil is probably obvious. It's the value of insulation, the addition of a big shielding layer of material and the air spaces within it, that allows the animal to retain the precious heat within its body and minimize heat loss by conduction into cool soil. It's the same story for the heavy blankets and down comforters that we put on top of ourselves sleeping in a cool bedroom in winter.

In an unusual case I found an interesting departure by three Merriam's kangaroo rats from the routine of staying in their deep-down winter nests all day. The surprise revealed itself to me during an unusual warm spell in late

January 1971 over a three-day period. The individuals involved were among those whose nests were so deep that I had not yet detected them with my Geiger counter on my morning searches. About noon on January 28, with the sun high in the sky and the air as calm and still as possible, temperatures were climbing into the mid 70s °F, and I was feeling physically very comfortable myself. This was a time of year when much colder, even freezing temperatures and gusting winds were more likely. Despite the beauty of this blue-sky day and the gorgeous profile of the snowy Sierra to the west, I was discouraged that I had been unable to locate any signal of these three kangaroo rats on my Geiger counter all morning long.

All of a sudden I picked up a loud signal, so hot I knew it was near the surface, and I zeroed in and marked it with red paint in the usual way. Found! And after that I found two more individual Merriam's burrow sites, with the animals similarly located near the surface. After later performing the usual calculations on the recorded intensity of the signals and measuring the soil temperature profile of each burrow hillock with the small probe, I discovered that all three of these animals were spending the afternoon in resting chambers only three to four inches below the surface in soil that had warmed up into the low to mid 60s °F. In the case of all three of these animals, the pattern continued for the next two days, when I was again unable to detect them in the morning (certainly resting in nests so deep that I could not pick up the signal), but then I picked them up again by midday when they came back up near the surface to enjoy an afternoon of "basking" in warm soil.

Of the burrow systems of the 60 kangaroo rats and pocket mice whose underground behavior I followed across the seasons of the year using gold tags, I excavated only a small proportion, because I felt that I could typify the general architecture of the systems, the tunnels and resting chambers, and the nests, with a smaller sample size. I did feel sorry for the individuals whose private home nests I disrupted and destroyed in the name of science, but those are the decisions one makes as a scientist. I saw some of my subjects hop away from my excavation sites into nearby burrows, perhaps as they would if they had just escaped an assault on their burrow by a badger, the great carnivoran predator best known for tearing into soil and ripping burrows and nests apart to dine on the resident rodents. Certainly my victims were not the first kangaroo rats who had to relocate and rebuild a nest in the middle of winter. I was happy when I caught many of them in the following months, as testament to the tough nature of wild animals and their ability to bounce back.

All together I excavated 13 nests of kangaroo rats in winter, before the breeding season began. I found interesting differences between chisel-toothed and Merriam's kangaroo rats, not only in the depth and location, but in the size and structure of the nests. Within each species the variation in nest size (and obviously the size of the dome-shaped soil cavity that held the nest) was very little. Nest building is certainly an innate behavior, resulting in a precise and consistent nest product, and most kangaroo rats, if they live so long, probably only build one or two winter nests in a lifetime. I initially measured each nest after I had scraped away sand from about one half of the domed cavity, and then I removed the nest for additional measurements and study in the lab.

The beautiful globular grassy nests of chisel-toothed kangaroo rats were about five inches high and six inches across, in diameter, weighing about 2.3 ounces. The smaller nests of Merriam's were just three and a half inches high and four inches across, weighing 1.6 ounces. These measurements, again, reflect the relative body-size difference between the two species, but it was interesting to realize that the actual weights of the nests slightly exceeded the weights of the animals. I don't believe I've ever slept with a bunch of winter blankets that weighed more than I do!

The nest chamber of each chisel tooth was enhanced beneath the grass nest by a layer of one or more inches of unusual bedding material—the discarded salty shavings from the saltbush leaves that are the main food of this species. Each nest had only a single little entrance hole that allowed the animal to squeeze into a small resting cavity centered within the whole globular structure. The size of the resting space looked to me to be about the size of the kangaroo rat if it were rolled up into a ball, resting. The chisel-tooth nests were neatly and exclusively constructed with the only native species of perennial grass in the area, Indian rice grass. The Merriams also mostly used this same grass, but they improvised by adding bits of fine fuzzy flower parts from two of the shrubs in the habitat. And one clever Merriam's kangaroo rat must have happened upon the leavings of a predator that had killed a small bird. Its nest contained nearly 100 small feathers, an excellent form of body insulation invented by birds some 150 million years ago and available to any opportunistic nest-building rodent in the meantime.

I used the nests that I collected for a lab investigation of captive kangaroo rats, whose metabolism I measured with and without natural nests. I found that the insulation value of a nest at an air temperature of 40°F allowed chisel-toothed kangaroo rats to reduce their resting metabolism by 21%, whereas the smaller Merriam's kangaroo rats reduced their metabolic rate by only 14% when occupying a natural nest.

I learned, from a few excavations in late spring, that females used their winter nests to give birth to their young. In a couple of burrows of female chisel tooths whose young had emerged and become independent, I later discovered the remnants of what had been an originally well-formed nest, located in the usual nest cavity, but all torn down and trampled by the busy activity of nursing and caring for the ambitious and curious young up to the point of their permanent departure from the nest.

I was thrilled to learn that kangaroo rats and pocket mice moved up and down in their burrows during the course of the day and as the seasons passed, and that their movements were tracking cycles of temperature in the soil. Hot and cold, up and down, finding the right place to be at the right time. I was pleased with the privilege of getting to know these underground spaces where kangaroo rats and pocket mice lived, slept, and gave birth to their young. Part of the awe that has stayed with me all these years is the realization that the desert underground is not a place where many of my fellow humans have ventured. It was just dirt, just sand, and just a common place, like so much of Earth's crust, out in pristine places that receive little or no direct human impact. I appreciate this underground world now whether I'm standing up on top of it, or thinking about what's down below, or if I were to make an imaginary journey through the miles of passageways that penetrate so much desert soil and allow so many little creatures to come and go, safely and quietly, within their burrows.

As I experienced my underground diggings, I found something mysterious about getting down into the soil. Each dig seemed like a fascinating new micro-spelunking adventure, a treasure hunt. Perhaps I imagined myself, much smaller, trying to navigate a labyrinth of downward descending tunnels. Might I be greeted by a kangaroo rat cousin of Stuart Little, the famous mouse with human characteristics introduced by E. B. White in 1945, the year I was born? Although my excavations revealed a great deal about the rodents in the place where they spend most of their lives, the ecological significance of the soil was more complex than just a provision of rodent housing. The darkness of the moist sand was penetrated by the roots of bushes whose leaves were photosynthesizing in the bright sunlight up above. On one dig I found a strange looking mole cricket walking along in a tunnel, and on another I saw wormy insect larvae around some roots. What else was going on in the soil?

Soil is both an interface and a medium that inspires an ode. Soil is where geology meets biology. Soil is a substrate for life. It's the surface of our planet. The desert soils into which I dug on the floor of the Owens Valley were largely sand and silt. The soil beneath the biggest hillocks that held the oldest shrubs seemed to be the richest. I sensed that the soil was alive. Water entered the soil when the sky provided. Some of the water sustained life. Other water escaped by evaporating from the surface. Seeds rested on the soil surface, and some got worked down into the top layer, waiting for their year, their moment. Dead leaves and other organic debris waited on the surface, decaying, decomposing, moving along through the carbon and nitrogen and mineral cycles, down into the soil. The rodent latrines I saw and smelled were part of this biogeochemistry. Roots pulled water and minerals from the soil. Invisible microbes participated in these living processes. Perhaps I smelled them, but I wasn't otherwise physically aware of their presence. Soil was the medium for all of this. All of these cycles led to the renewal of life.

10

MEETING THE BEETLES

BEING COOL IN A HOT DESERT

The most fun I ever had teaching college students was in my field courses. That was where it happened, in the field, especially when we camped out for an entire weekend to experience nature in action. In spring of 1978 as a new faculty member I was signed up to teach a zoology course called *Environmental Physiology* for the first time. The course was supposed to show how physiology and behavior contribute to the survival and ecological success of animals.

I decided the real thing would be to take the class out to eastern Washington's sagebrush country, out beyond the Cascade Mountains. I wanted the students to discover first-hand how physiology and behavior are part of ecology. I wanted them to watch real animals doing real things and to sit around a campfire at night and talk about what was going on out in nature.

The site I chose was Frenchman Coulee, a dry east-west mini-canyon that joins the Columbia River canyon as it runs from north to south through the center of the state. The walls of Frenchman Coulee are made of massive black crystalized volcanic formations that feature vertical columns of basalt. The open, sandy floor of the coulee supports eastern Washington's predominant natural plant association, the sagebrush steppe. The designation of steppe, an ecosystem not as extreme as most deserts, also means that grasses live among the shrubs. This landscape also includes delicate lichens and mosses that live on the soil and rocks, hanging on to dear life helped by moisture available during cooler parts of the year. Frenchman Coulee is notable for harboring iconic denizens of the desert such as rattlesnakes, scorpions, and black-widow spiders.

I also found out that I could expect an abundance of big black beetles in Frenchman Coulee as well—strange beetles of a charming and gentle sort that I'd gotten to know as a graduate student in California's deserts. These would become the creatures we investigated in the field course. As a graduate student I had seen these beetles ambling slowly across the desert. Sometimes they stopped and stood motionlessly. Other times they performed their classic headstand, with tip of the abdomen pointing to the sky while emitting a peculiar aromatic signal-odor from a solution of chemicals known as quinones that was secreted from the beetle's rear end. Entomologists recognized this as a defensive behavior. These beetles also surprised me occasionally by appearing inside the small box traps I used for capturing kangaroo rats. The traps would smell of the slightly noxious, but to me nonetheless rather fragrant quinones. I would reach in, grab the insect between my thumb and forefinger, pull it out, and watch its six long legs all cycling in air. As I set the beetle onto the ground, the churning legs propelled the insect on its way across the desert floor.

These common desert insects are darkling beetles (family Tenebrionidae), which, as beetles go, can be pretty big, measuring up to an inch and a half long and weighing up to two grams. That makes the biggest of these beetles as heavy as the smallest of all birds—several species of hummingbirds—and the smallest of all mammals—several species of shrews, which are not rodents but members of the insectivore lineage. I was amused by the appearance of the beetles' slow and rather ungraceful movement, perhaps owing to their unusually long legs. Darkling beetles don't fly. They don't have wings. In fact, the two halves of the hard covering on their back (the elytra, which are the wing covers of all the beetles that fly) are fused down the midline, forming a solid shell that makes a darkling beetle as tough as a tank, protecting it from predators and from loss of body water. As vegetarians, darkling beetles seek out fresh or decaying vegetation, flowers, fruits, and seeds to eat.

I had become curious about the daily activity behavior and internal physiological clock of these beetles because I had seen them out and about both day and night. As a postdoc, I spent a couple of years studying circadian rhythms, which added to my wondering about beetle activity rhythms. How was their activity being adjusted between day and night, or was it adjusted at all, just random? The regulation of body temperature was another aspect of physiology and behavior that attracted me—the differences between so-called cold-blooded and hot-blooded animals. What patterns of daytime and nighttime environmental temperature might be relevant to how the beetles decide when to be active? It seemed that by combining some questions about circadian rhythms and body temperature, we would have our hands plenty full of opportunities to do some field research that represented the goals of our course.

Somehow I got the course started, after working ahead of time to prepare lectures and all the logistics for the first field trip. A few more than twenty students made up the class, mostly undergraduate seniors, and about a quarter were graduate students. Jan, my teaching assistant, was an ornithologist interested in physiology, and naturally he loved birding. He had moved west for graduate study from his native coastal Massachusetts. Another grad student, from Vermont, had introduced himself ahead of time and declared his interest in physiology as it relates to making measurements of physical conditions in the microenvironments where animals live. He had studied civil engineering and ecology in Boston and was known familiarly as Swifty, a nickname his mother gave him. Swifty spent a lot of time with me before the course began and helped to obtain and organize equipment that we would use for all the meteorology measurements. I have always found graduate students to be great colleagues, helpers, and friends.

We gathered quite a bunch of amusing gadgets: thermistors (temperature-sensitive resistors) on the end of wires that plugged into an electronic box to measure air temperature, a psychrometer (to measure humidity), an anemometer (to measure wind speed), and three kinds of radiometers (to measure different components of solar radiation: direct, reflected, and net radiation). Some of these could be carried around; others were mounted on tripods. Finally to measure the internal body temperature of beetles, we built some thermocouples (very thin paired copper and alloy wires, soldered together at the tip) that plugged into another kind of electronic box.

I'm looking back now over the time span of nearly four decades since my experience with the desert beetle physiology class at the beginning of my career and a formative time professionally. I believe that my deep memory of this time is grounded in the place where my students and I spent time in nature, on the dusty floor of Frenchman Coulee. It was the smell of sagebrush, the feel of warm winds, and the sight of beetles moving around in the sagebrush, where we met them as they let us observe their private lives. The memory is strong because I formed an attachment to Frenchman Coulee and the beetles, and I believe the students formed the same attachment — a connection we all shared.

The late 1970s were primitive years, before microcomputers and data loggers became readily available to implement automated data recording. We had to turn on our instruments, take visual readings from dials and gauges, and write them down on data sheets on clipboards. Thinking back about that now, in the second decade of the twenty-first century, the experience seems much longer ago than I would guess from the freshness of my personal memories.

The students were all abuzz after lunch on Friday, April 7, as they swarmed onto the zoology department loading dock to deposit their backpacks, sleeping bags, and tents. Jan and I got help from the students with the scientific gear, camp stoves, lanterns, five-gallon water containers, pots and pans, ice chests and finally the groceries purchased by the food committee. Yelling, laughing, tossing frisbees, playing hacky sack — those things were always going on when the students were waiting for the next action. We loaded everything and everybody into three vans and headed off in caravan mode, in hopes of staying within some proximity of one another as we drove across Lake Washington on the floating bridge that heads eastward toward the Cascade Mountains. Honking, head-light flashing, and hand waving were the means of communicating between vans, since this was long before cell phones, texting and electronic distraction.

Within little more than an hour we reached Snoqualmie Pass, just over 3,000 feet elevation, with plenty of winter's snow still showing in the alpine zone. Here we began our descent through the forests that thinned out into open country and the highest fingers of sagebrush, bitterbrush, and rabbitbrush that extended up onto the lower Cascade slopes. A linear corridor of trees continued downward along the Yakima River at roadside, and we rolled down into open rangeland holding cattle in the Ellensburg Basin. We made good time as we approached the Columbia River, about two and a half hours from Seattle. I narrated the ride in my van, with remarks about how eastern Washington differs from the west: summers hotter and drier, and winters colder than on the west. And the precipitation gradient: only about eight inches a year out in the dry sagebrush country, in contrast to three feet in Seattle and as much as nine feet up on the west slope near the pass.

Crossing the great Columbia River gives pause for reflection, as one senses its might and the vast lands from which it collects its waters: seven western states and adjoining British Columbia. The big river delivers more water into the Pacific Ocean than any other river in North or South America. Crossing the bridge and leaving the river at our back, we arrived in the province of the beetles — the arid, channeled scablands of rock, sand, and sage that comprise Washington's Columbia Plateau.

I always felt that the rather ugly word "scablands" was something of a shame for a landscape that I find so lovely. The scabby designation has to do with the scouring out of a former soil-rich landscape by a series of floods, going back as long as 1.5 million years ago, associated with ice and melt-waters that were dammed up by glaciers and periodically broke loose. The original volcanic rock goes back nearly 18 million years, when it began oozing up from Earth's core, forming sheets greater than a mile thick in places, but which contributed over millions of years to soil formation and eventually a rich landscape. Probably the greatest loss of soil occurred near the end of the last glaciation, around 15,000 years ago, when Lake Missoula, in western Montana, broke loose from behind a prong of glacial ice to release a cataclysmic flood that scoured out the remaining soil held on top of the volcanic rocks of eastern Washington, leaving, in one geologist's view, a "scabbed" landscape.

I continued my geological narrative as we neared the end of our ride. The scouring out of the channeled scablands by the Missoula Flood was so extensive and powerful that some of the soil was delivered all the way down to Oregon's since-then fertile Willamette Valley. I heralded that as perhaps Washington's greatest gift ever to Oregon and added that it was personally meaningful to me because all four of my great-grandfathers settled in the Willamette Valley in the late nineteenth century and grew foods for their families on that soil.

We were approaching Frenchman Coulee, just a few miles east of the Columbia River, on a side road that led back from the interstate highway toward the river. This place and the other similarly scoured-out dry canyons scattered across the Columbia Plateau are known as coulees, from a French word referring to flow. We made a gradual descent on the roadway carved out along the south wall. The floor of the coulee, at an elevation of only 827 feet above sea level, stretched down below on our right across about half a mile of sagebrush scrub, at the end of which the north wall was facing back toward us. Frenchman Coulee opened to the Columbia River canyon only about a mile from our expected field site. Just for fun, we continued driving all the way to the river, at the end of the pavement, then turned around back up into the coulee. We edged our vans over the road shoulder and onto a rough dirt track that crossed the bottom of the coulee toward our site. Dust rose up from the tires and coated the second and third vans behind us as we drove slowly and peered out at the sagebrush-dominated habitat. Ahead, we could see dune formations against the north wall of the coulee that resulted from the strong south winds that carried sand up from the river's bank. We slowed, pulled into a spot where previous campers had left a fire circle, stopped, and turned off the engines.

The doors popped open. Shouts of joy and grunts emerged from the vans as everyone got out to explore our coulee. Everybody fanned out to see what they could see. We lifted our heads to look up to the top of the 300-foot basalt cliff above us. Some of the students scrambled up a slope and attempted to get up on a rock ledge. Others rambled around the sagebrush down below.

I strolled around with the students and watched as everyone discovered their first darkling beetle. With its slow and deliberate pace, a darkling beetle out cruising on a cool late afternoon in early spring is not going to run away from you. Some students were tempted to bend down and pick up a beetle—a titillating experience to let it walk in the sensitive palm of your hand. They also touched the beetle's back to feel the hard protective shell formed by the two fused elytra. They watched the antennae wiggle, as the beetle responded to the surface of the unusual human hand. A few students got to see and smell the release of the quinone chemical from the tip of a beetle's abdomen, an accompaniment to the head-down-tail-up posture assumed by the threatened beetle.

Most of the eight darkling beetle species we eventually identified belonged to the genus *Eleodes*, and one of the most abundant somehow quickly became the class favorite, the clown beetle, *Eleodes hispilabris*. Weighing a good half a gram and measuring an inch in length, with a series of about 15 lengthwise bumpy ridges running along the elytra, it was pleasantly sizable to grab and to enjoy holding in your hand. Not knowing all the species names and identifications at the start, we designated them temporarily as Species A, Species B, etc., and then took examples of each back to Seattle for identification by entomologist experts.

We had planned to use today's remaining hours to get organized and comfortable and to make some preliminary observations. We would wait until tomorrow morning to begin our formal observations. It was late afternoon, and the sun would be setting above the western horizon above the Columbia River gorge shortly after 6 o'clock standard time, since we had only passed the equinox a couple of weeks earlier. A few of the most serious camper types in the class eventually returned dragging pieces of old sagebrush trunks or branches, ready to start the woodpile for tonight's campfire.

I gathered us together and issued a few suggestions for setting up our study area. A big football-field-sized area below camp and to the west would serve to conduct our hourly count of active beetles. A corresponding, independent area of identical habitat to the east would be available for us to rove around at any time to observe beetles and to capture them for body temperature measurements. Not far from our main social area—kitchen and campfire— we would set up the instrumentation for our weather station. Places in among the bushes and on soft sand, just east and west of camp and just uphill beneath the bluff, would be great for tents, or for sleeping spots for those, like myself, who would just be rolling out a sleeping bag on a pad on a ground cloth. Then of course the women's and men's latrines, over here, and over there. Take the shovel along when you have serious business to conduct.

I invited those who had established their sleeping spots to join in setting up the weather station, and in marking out the 100-meter-long census field, eight lanes wide, for what would become our hourly ten-minute-long "beetle walks," as we came to call them. For this big grid, we used a measuring tape and a compass to mark off a 100-meter-long rectangle, some stakes to pound into the ground at each end for the lanes across the field, and some big old sticks we found to mark the far end of the field. Meanwhile, the dinner cooking team was ready to assume their duties due to the social, if not nutritional importance of the evening meal on a campout.

I don't recall what we ate for dinner that first night, but the camp fare in general was simple, as on many such camping trips I took with students in the 1970s and 1980s — most everybody would eat anything, and it was just cheap but decent food. How about spaghetti or a chicken stew, and an iceberg lettuce salad with a bottle of grocery-store dressing? Vegetarianism and hyper-foody philosophy had not yet gained a strong foothold, though we dealt with special needs as necessary. Students drank water from their personal canteens or cups that they filled from our five-gallon containers. No fancy, flip-spout personal water containers or store-bought plastic water bottles in those days. Lunches were pretty much sandwiches, based on cheese, lunch meats, and peanut butter and jelly, so everyone could make their own. Throw in some apples and oranges or grapes. All this was supplemented with the students' personal supplies of chips, pretzels, and candy bars, not to mention the beer and wine they brought along to make the dinner and campfire time a bit more jolly. Breakfasts were simply coffee, tea, or hot chocolate, cereal or toast, and occasionally a more leisurely batch of pancakes. The morning and evening meals always involved the eternal Coleman stoves — filling tanks with fuel, pumping up the cylinders, lighting the burners, and re-pumping the cylinder. The same fuel system applied to the Coleman lanterns that provided camp atmosphere and illumination after dark. This was all a familiar routine for most of the students I met in my field courses in that era.

We got the campfire going before dinner, initially more for social reasons than for warmth, but that was appreciated later as the evening chilled. We had plenty of conversation about what was your hometown, what other courses were you taking, and how's the professor? The composition of the group around the fire regularly mixed and remixed, in part influenced by the shifts of which way the smoke was blowing. Much of the talk involved the whole group in a single conversation. I occasionally got in a few words about tomorrow's plans and the need to identify the first group of eight to conduct the morning's first beetle count. Gradually everyone decided when to hit the sack, accompanied with a good-night valedictory and a comment about how little sleep he or she had last night due to studying, writing a paper, or partying. Then there were always the campfire night owls who lingered and kept feeding the fire, extending the last quiet conversations of profound philosophy and the meaning of life on to midnight as the fire died down.

Jan and Swifty and I were the first up, before 5 a.m. My mind was buzzing with all the logistics we needed to get going: starting the weather station at 5 a.m., getting people to walk around and look for beetles as soon as they crawled out of their sacks, launching our hourly beetle counts, and measuring body temperature of individual beetles. The sky had clouded up overnight and thereby protected us from an extreme chill, but the first air temperatures we observed, in the lower 40s Fahrenheit, were enough to warrant a morning campfire. The first, eager early-birds got out of the sack and rummaged around to make coffee. Once we started our research routine, we always had data to collect, and so meals and snacking just continued throughout the day as possible, with some people eating while others were out observing or making measurements.

Swifty helped to set up the voltmeter and various electronic boxes that connected to the wires coming from the radiometers and temperature sensors. We positioned the instruments together at a weather station, so that a couple of people could take care of the hourly readings and clip-board entries once we showed them how. Everyone was supposed to understand the operation and significance of all the equipment.

Through everyone's initial searching for beetles in the early morning chill and intermittently congregating around the heat of the fire, nobody had yet seen a beetle, so we felt confident that their activity had not yet begun. We decided to conduct the first ten-minute count at 7 a.m., just after the hourly weather station data were collected. I called out for volunteers, before the hour, to come over and line up in the eight staked-out lanes of our 100-meter-long grid. Later, as this became a routine, I would just shout "beetle walk," and others would echo the call, "beetle walk." That became all we had to do to reassemble a new group of eight observers each hour.

I directed the first few beetle walks, with my eye on a stopwatch and the goal of adjusting our pace so that each walk would last ten minutes, consisting of five minutes moving 100 meters westbound, turning around, and five minutes returning eastbound. All eight of us kept more-or-less abreast of one another at the defined pace. We could see the tall sticks we had planted yesterday at the far west end, so we knew how far we had to go, and I called out "faster" or "slower" depending on what proportion of the 100 meters we had covered and the time showing on the stopwatch. Each person was instructed to watch the ground with the greatest possible concentration across a lane of about 5 meters width, and each person kept track mentally or made notes as necessary of the number and kind of beetles seen. When we turned around at the far end, each of us shifted over to an adjacent 5-meter lane for the return trip. Upon return to the east end and crossing the finish line, each observer reported to the captain the numbers and kinds observed, and someone recorded the results in columns on the data sheets, followed, on the right, by a column for adding up the total number of beetles.

We counted 20 beetles on the 7 a.m. beetle walk, representing a thorough ten-minute scan of about two acres of sagebrush desert by sixteen eyeballs, that is, eight human observers. We had beetle data! Air temperature just above the ground, in other words at the height where beetles were active, had risen to about 50 degrees Fahrenheit. (Of course we recorded temperatures on all our instruments in degrees Celsius, °C, by standard scientific protocol, but I am generally using the more familiar Fahrenheit, °F, to relate this story.) We had just discovered that some of the beetles had begun their daily foraging activities, and we had also established the protocol of the beetle walks that would become the routine backbone of our ability to answer the question: when were these beetles active? Only by repeating this procedure over and over could we achieve a full picture. We would continue throughout this day, and again tomorrow. And we would return again, in May, to repeat our observations and look for any possible shift that might occur in time of activity as the season progressed.

As this first day progressed, we sensed that the heavy cloud cover was slowing the rate at which the habitat was going to warm up, but nonetheless by 9 and 10 o'clock we counted more than 100 beetles each hour. Air temperature just above the ground, at beetle height, had reached 68°F, and we, the scientists, were feeling perfectly comfortable now ourselves. Under continued cloud cover, air temperature did not rise much above midday readings in the low 70s °F, and hourly beetle activity continued, but with a gradual decline in numbers, throughout the afternoon.

Beginning after the 7 a.m. beetle walk, we used the interim periods between beetle walks to search the adjoining easterly grid (so as not to disturb the beetle-walk grid) for beetles whose various behaviors we could observe or whose body temperatures we could measure. During the cooler, earlier part of the morning we observed some interesting beetle behavior on the easterly grid—a number of individuals that moved out into the open soil in full sunlight and assumed a head-down and tail-up posture. And then we noticed that these beetles were orienting their backs to incoming sunshine (or in technical lingo, to incoming direct solar radiation). These beetles, in cool morning air, consistently oriented their backs directly toward the sun's rays arriving from low in the eastern sky in order to catch the sun's rays and warm themselves up for activity. This was sunbathing at its best, and the beetles were assuming what we imagined to be a rather elegant, yoga-like pose to accomplish that goal.

We needed to answer an important question: what was the normal range of body temperatures for the beetles when they were active? Knowing that would allow us to interpret the presence and absence of beetle activity, as determined on the beetle walks, in relation to the body temperatures the beetles could achieve at any particular time of day or night, depending on prevailing environmental conditions. I led a small team out, usually with two or three others at a time, to develop and then carry out our routine for measuring beetle body temperatures. We obtained the measurement by probing the internal thorax (middle body segment) of the beetles with a very thin hypodermic needle into the tip of which I had glued a super thin pair of thermocouple wires that harmlessly registered the temperature a few millimeters inside the beetle's body. To accomplish this we walked around until we spotted an active beetle. I grabbed the beetle off the ground with my right hand and placed it in the insulated tips of a broad forceps held in my left hand. I then used my right hand to insert the tip of the needle through the beetle's chitin exoskeleton. A student held the electronic box, activated the circuit switch, focused on the needle dial, and reported the temperature reading. Another team member wrote the temperature on the clipboard, along with the time and species name. To assure accuracy of the beetle's original temperature, we only accepted a reading if we could obtain it within five seconds of picking the beetle up. Next we recorded three temperatures with our probe where we found the beetle: soil surface (in open sun and in nearby shade) and air at the height of the beetle, just above the ground. We kept each beetle in a labeled plastic vial to return to the university for weighing and species identification. We continued this routine hourly through early evening when beetle activity ceased. On this trip we successfully measured the body temperature of 48 active beetles.

We would have to accumulate a lot of these body temperature readings to analyze the overall pattern of range and average, and that number eventually reached 255 measurements for the entire project. That allowed us to conclude that the body temperatures of 96.5% of all our beetles fell between 10°C and 30°C, coincidentally and conveniently round numbers on the Celsius scale which translate to 50°F to 86°F, with an average body temperature of 69°F. This very important range of 50°F to 86°F is what we needed to know in order to define the natural range of body temperatures for the full course of the natural seasons of beetle activity at which the beetles were willing and able to perform their normal activities.

The normal range of beetle body temperatures over all seasons can be summarized this way: below 50°F they were apparently unable to be active; between 50°F and 86°F they were generally active, moving around and foraging; and above 86°F they were apparently unable or unwilling to remain active. The existence of this observed normal temperature range suggests that the beetles exercise behaviors to maintain themselves within that range and to avoid exceeding 86°F. The 86°F natural upper limit of beetle temperature is interesting to us as humans, because it is about 13°F below our own human operating body temperature of 98.6°F. Another interesting comparison with human comfort is that the average beetle body temperature of 69°F is near what we consider comfortable room temperature in modern human dwellings. But alas, we humans, along with other mammals, have a high and fairly constant body temperature and a corresponding high rate of energy metabolism, designating us as endotherms or homeotherms, to use two technical terms. Beetles, in contrast, are "cold-blooded" insects who must locate themselves behaviorally in microclimate situations that allow them to achieve their own appropriate operating body temperature. They do not generate enough heat with their internal metabolism to heat themselves up, warranting the technical labels of ectotherms or poikilotherms.

We continued our hourly collection of weather data. Our instrumentation and data were more complex than the minimal information obtained at the simplest US Weather Bureau stations of the time, since we recorded various air temperatures from the surface to a height of 2 meters, humidity, wind speed, and atmospheric radiation in all its components. One of our goals was to use all these data to develop a model to predict the body temperatures of beetles on various days of their natural activity season. We eventually did that successfully, but that required a complex and lengthy analysis.

By sunset we were finding no more beetles, neither on our beetle walks nor on other searches around the habitat. That was our cue to move forward with a good social evening of dinner, campfire, and the usual jolliness and occasional nonsense. As the night progressed, the sky cleared and we experienced a much colder night than the previous night, with bright stars and no moon showing.

Getting up Sunday morning before 5 a.m., we found freezing cold air, right at 32°F. But with this morning's totally clear sky, the sun warmed up the floor of Frenchman Coulee much faster than under yesterday's clouds. This was a lesson in day-to-day variation in habitat micrometeorology. We pulled off our first beetle walk at 6 a.m. and found no beetles at all. That was important to establish negative data in this case, demonstrating a lack of activity. By 7 a.m. we counted the first few beetles, and in the next couple of hours still more. But by midday the soil surface had heated up to over 86°F, and beetle activity was suspended, rather than continuing as it had throughout yesterday's cloud-covered afternoon. It occurred to us, as we reckoned with the difference in today's activity, that we might look for beetles in the shaded litter beneath big bushes, and indeed we found a few. This showed that although it was too hot to move around actively in the open, a few beetles remained above ground in the shade. Even so, the measured body temperatures of the beetles we found in the shade were near the upper limit of 86°F. Once we documented the end of activity, we packed up our camp because it was time to head for home.

We had a good ride home, recounting the glories of our accomplishments. Everyone had gotten to know the little black insects who walked around on the sand in the sagebrush. Our data collection system was working. Conversations grew quieter toward the end of our three-hour ride, as weary souls found themselves asleep in the back seats. We had already scheduled the second trip for the first weekend of May, a month away, and we could now imagine what it might be like, both for us as a class and for the beetles whose lives we wanted to discover more thoroughly.

Our second field trip a month later, in early May, was preceded by heightened enthusiasm and expectations — a seeming mandate that the second trip had to be better than the first. The snacks and treats would be more and better. Chocolate bars, marshmallows, and graham crackers would be combined to build s'mores around the campfire. I was uninformed, however, of everything else the class and the dinner committee had planned.

We left the zoology loading dock promptly in early afternoon and found ourselves in the bottom of Frenchman Coulee in time to pull off the first beetle walk at 5 p.m. The warmth of air, smell of sagebrush, and feel of dust and sand brought us back to the mood we had experienced a month earlier, except that now it was warmer. The first squad of eight counted 13 beetles moving around in the late afternoon, with air temperatures in the low 70s °F and soil surface temperatures in the low 80s. The ground holds the heat of the day for a prolonged period, whereas the air loses heat and declines in temperature more rapidly. After observing a few more beetles at 6 p.m. and 7 p.m., we saw our last beetles, only three in number, at 8 p.m., when environmental temperatures had dropped to just above 50°F, the lower limit of active beetle body temperature. The air continued to cool as the evening ensued.

The scientific observations of our first evening back in the coulee were to a great extent upstaged by a dinner event of epic proportion that unfolded as we continued our beetle walks and recording of weather data. Our volunteer, self-appointed, executive chef Dave was joined by Becky to plan the most elaborate meal presentation I have ever experienced on a campout. Over the coming year on further occasions in my lab and around the department, Dave revealed himself to be something of a renaissance man, which accounts for the charm he added to our experience in Frenchman Coulee.

Dave and Becky's production far surpassed the simplicity of field-trip cooking by which I typified our first trip. They had made an excursion to Seattle's Pike Place Market to obtain a batch of whole salmon. Back at Becky's apartment they cleaned the fish, leaving heads on, stuffed them with lemon wedges and butter, stitched them closed with dental floss, and wrapped them in foil boats for transport to the field and cooking over the campfire on a grill. They also prepared an exquisite chilled cucumber soup ahead of time and rounded out the menu with a pleasantly herbed pilaf preparation on the Coleman stove. Dave and Becky provided a full explanation of the sophisticated details of their preparations as they busied themselves and other helpers around the Frenchman Coulee kitchen.

The meal was a complete surprise to me—the professor kept in the dark. Yet more surprises awaited, with the appearance of a white folding party table and four matching chairs that emerged from one of the vans. In turn, the table was adorned with a white tablecloth, formal dinnerware, two candlesticks, and a large wooden pepper mill. The incongruous sight of this display on the dusty soil among scattered sage bushes and backed by the gorgeous columnar basaltic walls of Frenchman Coulee could be considered surreal, but for this group, as wine bottles were opened, this was just college fun, and pretty silly at that. It was insisted that I come to the table for the first seating, not at all clear whether this whole thing was an adulation or a parody of my professorial status. Other seatings followed, and everyone dined with pleasure. The cooling desert air filled with warm laughter, and the story of the funny dinner was repeated around the fire, and for weeks to come.

The serious scientific mission was not forgotten, and somehow I think it was being celebrated with the fancy dining experience in a beautiful natural setting. Dave had more for us. Not to retire on the mere glory of the dinner, renaissance Dave repurposed the dinner table, produced a deck of cards, and announced the Frenchman Coulee Rolling Bridge Tournament, over which he presided at the table under lantern light. Those with bridge experience were invited to take a turn at the table, as the evening advanced. Gradually each of us reached our threshold, and we retired to our sleeping bags.

The new day began about 4 a.m., when Jan, Swifty and I crawled out of our sacks to launch the coffee, the meteorology equipment, and the deeply sleeping students. The air was chilled, in the upper 30s °F, and we found no beetles active at 5 a.m. By 6 a.m. the sun had risen and air warmed to 50°F, and we found our first two beetles on the 6 a.m. beetle walk. At 7 a.m. we counted a dozen beetles, as temperatures climbed into the 60s °F and moved quickly upward toward mid range of the beetle comfort zone. Strong activity continued for a couple of hours but then declined to only two beetles at 10 a.m., and by 11 a.m. there were no more beetles. That was a short morning for the beetles! Over the next five hours, through 3 p.m., with air temperatures climbing into the upper 80s and soil temperatures exceeding 100°, we conducted our beetle walks and found no beetles. The middle of the day appeared to be unsuitable for the beetles.

The mid- and late-morning sunshine delighted everyone, now clad in shorts and t-shirts. During the five-hour mid-day absence of beetles on our beetle walks, we continued on lookout, nonetheless, for beetles, searching independently both in open areas and under shaded litter beneath bushes. These observations confirmed that the beetles had truly checked out. We enjoyed the exploration time as an opportunity to find out what else was going on in the coulee. Green shoots of grasses and small desert annual plants had proliferated to full size by this point in spring. The flowers were variously colored with yellows, pinks, reds, and blues that contrasted with the freshness of their green foliage. A few students hiked up to the head of the coulee, where a dashing cascade of water descended over the basaltic face, carrying the remnants of winter accumulation to splash into a sink hole on the coulee floor. Everyone found time for a bite of lunch, as they drifted in and out of camp.

We discovered more animal inhabitants, including three kinds of lizards, and we saw quite a lot of them. Smallest and most common was the side-blotched lizard, mostly about 2–3 inches long, and with a prominent identifying bluish-black blotch just behind the front legs. A close relative of the side-blotched lizard, an inch or so longer was the aptly named sagebrush lizard, which is one of the so-called blue-belly lizards, with a few bluish scales on top and lots of brighter blue along both sides of the belly. Very different in body form, with a broad, rounded body outline, were the "horny toads," of course not toads, but proper lizards, common here in Washington's sagebrush, and officially known as the short-horned lizard, getting up to 3–4 inches in length. Lots of the side-blotched lizards climbed rocks and ran around bushes. Sagebrush lizards and horned lizards were mostly on the ground out in the sagebrush habitat.

The reptile that gained the strongest attention, loud shouts in fact, was the western rattlesnake. We spotted several of them, the only rattler species that lives in Washington and correspondingly the most common and widespread species throughout western North America. With each sighting, loud calls erupted from the discoverers, and nearby students all hurried to see for themselves. These were big, heavy-bodied snakes, on the order of three to four feet long, and at a safe distance we came to enjoy watching them. Everyone was aware of the dangerous venom these snakes can inject with their long front fangs, contained in the powerful jaws of the wide, triangular-shaped head. Generally the rattlers remained quietly coiled beneath bushes or near rocks where we found them, but on a couple of occasions a bit of curiosity-inspired provocation with a long stick elicited the signature buzzing sound from the set of hard rattle segments at the tip of the snake's tail.

Jan was our bird authority, usually keeping his binoculars handy. Everyone got to identify the conspicuous meadowlarks in our coulee, with their yellow breast and signature black V-band up toward the throat. Moving around on the ground in search of insects and seeds, they were probably among the birds that commonly preyed on darkling beetles. We also spotted the sage sparrow, a well-known associate of the namesake shrub habitat. In general the birds down in the bottom of the coulee remained inconspicuous during midday heat, and most of our sightings were earlier morning or late afternoon.

We eventually found signs of predation on our beetles, in the form of bits of sun-bleached beetle exoskeleton around the holes of black widow spiders, and in the scats of coyotes. Rodents, lizards, and ground-feeding birds are among the critters best known to eat darkling beetles out in the sagebrush country.

By the 4 p.m. beetle walk we finally observed beetles again, six this time, as air temperatures dropped back down into the comfort zone. This was the beginning of a late-afternoon and early-nighttime pulse of activity that lasted for six hours until we counted our last beetles at 10 p.m., about two hours after sunset, when air and soil temperatures again fell below the 50°F lower limit for beetle activity. During the evening beetle walks we used our Coleman lanterns and some flashlights, so that each observer could stare at the light-colored, dusty ground around and among the bushes in order to see any beetles that were moving around as we passed by.

During the ongoing hourly beetle walks and weather recordings of the early evening, we enjoyed another fine dining experience on the fly, ducking in and out of camp as duty called. Dave and Becky brought a big package of top round, which they seasoned and browned at the stove, adding some hearty burgundy. They simmered this to yield a proper boeuf bourguignon, which they served over egg noodles. For a lighter touch, they prepared a fine green salad. Although the element of surprise was gone for me after the previous evening's experience, we all remained amused with the further hyperbole of elegant cuisine in the sagebrush setting. We had another great evening in our communal camp.

The next morning's activity, on Sunday, was initiated both by students and beetles on a schedule essentially identical to that of the previous day. We worked for the remainder of the second morning until we had confirmed the disappearance of all the beetles, which happened again as the environment heated up to an intolerable extreme for the beetles.

Our overall May results contrasted sharply with the single, long daytime bout of beetle activity that we had observed a month earlier in April. The striking pattern that the beetles showed us in May amounted to two separate activity periods — one from dawn to mid morning and the other from late afternoon until early evening, separated by a five-hour mid-day hiatus of no activity. We obtained an additional 85 measurements of body temperatures of active beetles on this trip, which we eventually determined were not significantly different on average from the body temperatures of beetles in April. Thus these beetles were showing themselves not to be creatures of clock-bound habit with a fixed daily schedule of activity, but rather they were fixed to a particular range of body temperatures, the thermal window of 50–86°F, whenever that could be achieved. Our discoveries so far were exciting for us as a class, but the spring quarter would be over in a few weeks for the students. I wanted to know what would happen to the beetles later, in the heat of summer and then again when autumn brought cooler temperatures.

I was thinking it would be exciting to continue the beetle observations on into the summer and fall. In addition to the behavioral and physiological discoveries we made about the beetles during the spring, I liked the sense of the connection we had formed with the beetles and with Frenchman Coulee. The beetles were doing something that fell outside the simple model of being strictly day-active or strictly night-active. Swifty and I talked about extending the project. He was enthusiastic and hoped we could do something with the masses of data we were accumulating on temperature, wind speed, humidity, and direct and reflected components of short-wave and long-wave solar radiation. Those weather data should be useful for modeling the behavior of the beetles at different seasons.

I started checking with the students from our class

and with other graduate students in our department to ask who would like to go on a summer field trip, and then maybe again in the fall. One of the undergraduates from the beetle course was Terry, who had also taken my field course on natural history of mammals the previous spring. She was interested in physiology and was working in my lab. She was in! Word of the culture of our class field trips had resonated around the department. I kept a few pet beetles in a terrarium in my lab, and visitors had come by to meet the strange little black creatures. On the wall above my desk, visitors also saw a bright eight-by-ten color photo of a clown beetle doing a head-stand out in Frenchman Coulee. Soon enough we had a small team of beetle fans, both veterans of the spring course and neophytes, who signed on for the summer and fall trips.

Our summer beetle gang departed for Frenchman Coulee as July was turning to August. I made sure to care for all the logistic details of both science and camping, but of course we would never again eat as fancily as we did with chef Dave. We were expecting sizzling hot weather out in eastern Washington, and that's exactly what we found. As we descended over the east slope of the Cascades, heat grew in the van, which lacked air-conditioning, typical of university vehicles in the 1970s, and we drove with open windows.

We were happy to return down the sloping paved road along the south wall of the coulee and look across to our site over near the north wall. We talked about this as our place and liked the sense of familiarity. Air temperature as we arrived in late afternoon was in the mid 80s °F. To avoid the dust of the sagebrush flats, we rolled up the windows for the short drive across the coulee. It felt great to get out and walk around, looking up at the radiant surfaces of the basaltic columns. The day's heat had volatilized the strongly pungent oils in the sagebrush leaves that we smelled now.

Our first census was the 7 p.m. beetle walk, with still more than an hour remaining until sunset. The sun was lowering itself, and shadows lengthened on the east side of shrubs. With air and soil temperatures in the mid and low 80s °F, any active beetles should be operating within the upper end of their comfort zone. We were excited to find a robust beetle traffic count of 31 beetles at 7 o'clock. We had learned enough in May to suspect that we should remain on alert and keep doing beetle walks on into the summer night, using lanterns. We continued to obtain measurements of beetle body temperatures whenever we could manage.

Indeed we continued to find beetles out and about during the progression of the later evening. At 10 p.m. we still counted 12 beetles. We kept up the weather station measurements, and at midnight the soil surface and air just above the surface still remained comfortably in the low 60s °F. The walks at midnight and 2 p.m. revealed beetles still active, though in reduced numbers. To provide ourselves a little extra sleep, we skipped beetle walks at 1 a.m. and 3 a.m. It was not an easy instinct to get up out of a sleeping bag in the middle of the night in response to a noisy alarm clock, to pull on your clothes and boots, and to light a lantern so you could walk 100 meters west, turn around, and walk back 100 meters east looking for insects ambling around in the scrub. But we did it.

We must have been quite a sight slogging along in the dark, each person gazing at the illuminated ground just ahead, holding a lantern or strong flashlight high, glancing across occasionally at the other lights bobbing along in the dark of night. Terry appeared each time, ready to go, with her hair wrapped firmly in a bandana, and she once characterized our somber procession as a line of zombies combing the sagebrush. When Swifty got up for one of the walks and was pulling on his pants, he shouted a one-word announcement over a surprise next to his sleeping bag: "rattlesnake!" That certainly brought him, and all of us, to a full state of alertness.

Later, with dawn approaching, the 4 a.m. walk revealed a count of 9 beetles. A further increase to 18 beetles at both 5 and 6 a.m. showed us that morning was bringing on an increase in activity as the temperatures edged up above the overnight minimum in the upper 50s °F. But even this minimum summer overnight air temperature occurred within the normal comfort range for beetle activity, which corresponded with our beetle-walk observation of activity throughout all hours of the summer night. The morning increase in activity continued through 8 a.m., and that was all. By 9 a.m. we found no more beetles, which was not so surprising when we looked at environmental temperatures — air at beetle height already 90°F and soil surface a sizzling 117°F.

For the first couple of hours after beetles disappeared at 9 a.m., we continued to patrol around in the habitat, hoping to spot more beetles, perhaps one whose body temperature we could take, but we found none. This was a chance to see other critters, and the lizards were among those who remained active. We frequently found spiders, including black widows, whose identity we assured by flipping them over carefully with a little twig to confirm the red hour-glass spot underneath. Also in the leaf litter around shrubs we occasionally found scorpions. Watching a scorpion respond by probing at it gently with a small twig was like attending a weapons demonstration. The scorpion elevated itself at attention on its legs and erected the tip of stinger-bearing tail in a forward curving arc, a splendid and frightening display.

We also came to know with new fondness one of the smaller darkling beetle species that showed us a new way of moving around that we did not see in any of the others. This species, not a member of the more typical genus *Eleodes*, was *Eusattus muricatus*. In fact, the species had no common name, and the observant student John, who first noticed the behavior, dubbed this beetle the Volkswagen beetle, in part for the similar profile of its body to that of the classic German car. The VW insect was less than half an inch long. Its unusual behavior occurred when it climbed up or down the steeper sloping drifts of sand right around our camp. As sand grains trickled downward beneath its moving legs, the beetle simply swam into the loose sand and disappeared. This adeptness also earned *Eusattus* the well-deserved title of dune buggy. This species has been recognized scientifically as a habitat specialist, essentially living in association with wind-blown sand dunes in the deserts of western North America.

The hot summer daytime of the first day of August continued for a period of ten hours without any beetle activity at all. (In May the daytime period of inactivity was five hours.) The intense heat of midday and early afternoon dramatically fulfilled all our expectations for this trip to represent the hottest possible weather. Air temperatures in the shade of tall sagebrush remained in the range of 104 to 111°F, clearly far above the top of our observed range of normal beetle body temperatures at 86°F. Hotter still was the soil out in open sunshine, which reached a maximum of 150°F. The first beetles we sighted again after this ten-hour beetle time-out appeared in the early evening, which by coincidence was on our 7 p.m. beetle walk, the same hour at which we had arrived yesterday and counted our first beetles.

On our summer trip it was important to document beetle behavior for two full nights, even though that meant repeating the uncomfortable routine of waking up at intervals, getting out of the sack for another beetle walk, and relighting the lanterns at all hours of the night. It turned out the results of the second night very closely resembled the first night, and that's just the value added by repeating a sampling routine — confirming that observed behavior is typical. In summary, summer beetle activity occurred in one long continuous bout, mostly in the dark of night. It began just before sunset, showed an early evening pulse, backed off to a lower level that continued all night, and finally showed another strong pulse of activity that began before dawn and lasted for only a few hours after sunrise. On this trip we obtained an additional 54 measurements of active beetle body temperature, and as part of our bigger data set, these also showed no seasonal change in the comfort range of 50 to 86°F. The extreme distinction of summer activity was the complete absence of activity for ten hours of the daytime that was complemented by fourteen hours of mostly nocturnal and twilight activity.

We figured the early October trip would be our last, enough to document what the beetles did with the coming of fall and its cooler temperatures. Crossing the Cascades, we looked upward as we reached Snoqualmie Pass, where only the highest peaks were capped with remnants of last winter's snows. The coniferous trees showed the lush greens of a good summer growing season, and the vine maple understory was starting to show the reds and yellows that announce autumn. We breezed down through the transition to sagebrush and crossed the Columbia River.

As we descended into our coulee, we sensed the passage of seasonal time. The sagebrush landscape on the floor of Frenchman Coulee showed a soft gray color from leaves that were dulled by the bleaching sunshine of a harsh summer. But a bright new color stood out against the sagebrush tones—brilliant gold flowers at the tops of rabbitbrush, a member of the sunflower family. Compared to the dominance of sagebrush in the plant community, rabbitbrush was by far in the minority, and tended to live on the margins, in disturbed spots, but the striking color of its autumn flowers now made up for its less common occurrence. Rabbitbrush was aptly named in Latin, at the time of our beetle project, with the genus *Chrysothamnus*, reflecting the Greek root "chryso" for gold, which I found appealing. (Unfortunately in the mean time, well-meaning botanists performed a clever analysis that required them to strip the beautiful bush of its more colorful scientific name and substitute another. That's just the way science progresses on occasion.)

We enjoyed the familiarity of settling into our study site, as before. A comforting sign of the remoteness of our place was, once again, the lack of any clue as to human disturbance. The dunes and camping area seemed clean and unmolested. Our guide posts and stakes remained as we had placed them. During each of our stays we saw only occasional cars driving down the paved road into the coulee. No one ever drove across the dirt track to explore our area or inquire as to what we were doing. We were truly and happily out in the boonies.

We plunged right in with our first beetle walk at 4 p.m., a couple of hours before sunset, and with air temperatures in the mid range of beetle comfort. The 10 beetles we spotted in the first walk were surpassed in the 5 p.m. walk by even more beetles, but then the activity declined over the next couple of hours until we observed a complete absence of beetles by 8 p.m. and thereafter. During these first few hours we also found beetles in the adjoining habitat and collected more of the needed body temperature measurements.

The next morning's minimum air temperatures dropped to near 40°F, well below the typical 50°F minimum body temperature for active beetles. At 6 a.m. and again at 7 a.m. our beetle walks resulted in no beetles, despite the sun rising above the horizon. Finally at 8 a.m. we counted a couple of beetles, and then by 9 a.m., when temperature had increased to the mid 60s °F, we found 11 active beetles. During the intervals between the morning beetle walks, when we were walking around the easterly grid, we spotted individual beetles out in the open sunning themselves in the same yoga pose we had observed on cool, sunny mornings in spring. These individuals oriented their backs to the incoming sunshine by bowing their heads to the ground, facing the sun, and raising their abdomens up in the air, perpendicularly to incoming solar rays—the perfect basking posture. More and more beetles became active every hour throughout what turned out to be a mild, clear, sunny day. The warmest air we encountered all day, down near the soil surface at beetle height, reached the mid 80s °F, corresponding to the upper end of the beetle comfort zone. Even the hottest soil surface temperature, in early afternoon, reached only the lower 90s °F.

We became excited by a new behavioral observation involving just one of the smaller beetle species, which everyone noticed right away and continued to observe throughout our entire stay. Most of the beetles of all the other species were walking around as usual on the ground, but *Eleodes humeralis* was showing up in the tops of the rabbitbrush, two or three feet above ground, clinging to the tiny golden flowers at the tips of branches. Clearly, with twitching antennae and moving mouthparts, the small beetles were feasting on the clusters of dainty tubular flowers. It was fun for us to discover this exceptional situation—a feeding behavior that was apparently turned on by the presence of pungent golden flowers that attracted beetles of only one uniquely specialized species to climb up and seek a culinary treat available during just this one brief period of the year.

On our second evening we received an amusing weather surprise. A warm air mass moved into the area, and at 8 p.m. the air temperature, at about 60°F, was 10 degrees warmer than the previous night. That allowed the beetles to remain active in greater numbers and for a couple of hours longer than on the previous night.

The general conclusion from our October observations was that beetle activity had returned to a daily schedule like that of early springtime. Beetles conducted their activity over a single broad period of the daytime, basically between sunrise and sunset, but with a bit of delay at the beginning associated with cool early morning hours, and a small extension of activity into the early evening, after sunset, provided it was warm enough. We kept ourselves busy obtaining 68 new records of beetle body temperature over the three days we worked, which gave us a total for all four trips of 255 measurements of internal body temperature from early spring, late spring, summer, and early autumn. The overall statistical analysis we computed for all these data indicated no seasonal shift in the average (69°F) or range (50°F to 86°F) of body temperature preferred by the beetles.

Our walks around the coulee, our time spent watching individual beetles, our evening meals, and our campfires all seemed like a celebration. We shared the satisfaction of completing a series of new observations that would lead to a scientific publication. We also shared the personal satisfactions and delights that derived from the seasons of time we spent in Frenchman Coulee meeting darkling beetles. I believe that this happened because we were able to immerse ourselves in nature and pay attention to small and curious everyday creatures—how they came and went, day and night, as the seasons passed.

From the seasonal progression of our four field trips in Frenchman Coulee we were able to draw scientific conclusions about the natural body temperatures of darkling beetles and how that influenced the times of day and night when they were active. The natural range of body temperatures, 50–86°F, remained the same across the seasons and was relatively cooler than that of many other active insects. To achieve these cooler temperatures as a priority, the beetles adjusted the times when they were active. In the hot summer they were out in evening and morning twilight and at all hours of the night in between, never in mid-day heat. In early spring and fall we found them active throughout the day and scarcely at all at night.

In May we found an unusual intermediate pattern—two separate activity periods per day, one from dawn to mid morning and then a second activity period from late afternoon until early evening.

Our darkling beetles seemed to be masters of being cool, and not actually able to tolerate the higher body temperatures naturally experienced by some of the other insects. A review of scientific literature revealed that dragonflies, grasshoppers, bugs, butterflies, bees, and even other kinds of beetles operate at much higher body temperatures than darkling beetles—beyond 100°F and all the way up to 113°F. This range is way above the darkling beetle comfort zone, and even a good 15°F warmer than our own human body temperature of 98.6°F. Many of these hot-blooded insects are flyers, who achieve a higher metabolism and body temperature to crank up their muscles for flight, and along with that the hot-blooded insects just tolerate higher levels of body temperature, allowing them to remain active during the heat of summer daytime, when darkling beetles retire to underground shelter.

A lot of computation and analysis followed our data collection adventures in Frenchman Coulee. Swifty kept working with me for a couple of years to refine the data and develop a publishable report. We managed to refine the weather data into a sort of weather-forecasting model that could predict beetle body temperatures and times of activity. That was the fate of the science that we ended up publishing in the journal *Ecology*. That's what you do as a scientist.

Frenchman Coulee became a personal place for my students and me over the course of six months of natural seasonal change that occurred in 1978. We came to know the heat of the day, the bright blue sky, the columnar basalt walls, the sand dunes and dust on the sagebrush floor, and the clear night sky roof above us. We met lizards, snakes, scorpions, spiders, and beetles. All the organisms we found have become members of the sagebrush ecosystem over a lengthy period of geological and biological time that extends back beyond the entire history of our own human species on Earth. Although we did not experience that longer passage of time in the coulee—from the 18-million-year-ago formation of the basalt sheets through the more recent 15,000-year-ago scouring by the Missoula Flood—I believe that just knowing this deeper history as a scientific fact provides a feeling that we are a part of that whole, long history as well.

The beetle course taught me a lot about teaching and learning. I realize in the meantime that nature herself was doing the teaching. I had first begun to discover that in my personal experience as a graduate student beginning my research career. Through all of this I now know that my sense of discovery is sustained by the truth that emerges from being in nature and paying attention. Out in Frenchman Coulee I learned from my students, as I watched and listened to them. They too were finding the awe that comes with time spent in a natural place and what it can teach you.

11

THE PANDA'S MESSAGE

Cold mountain air, towering firs and spruce with
occasional stands of larch, sheer granite peaks with
white pockets of snow reflecting bright sunshine
under a clear blue sky—this was a delight. I was walking
with new friends above 8,000-feet elevation in a Chinese
forest whose cone-bearing trees, as well as birches and
poplars, reminded me of the closely related tree species from
the boreal forests of North America and Europe. I realized
that part of my joy over the beauty of these mountains in
western Sichuan Province was the feeling of familiarity that
came from recognizing the trees. This was my first visit to
Asia, 2001, and I was surprised to feel at home in a strange
place. A breeze pushed the mountain air, bracing and clean.

I breathed it in deeply. A powerful river crashed down the mountainside, raising a din of white noise, as the water broadcast a visible spray that misted off big boulders in the steep river course below us. Rhododendrons along the river bank, with showy flowers of magenta, white, and lavender, added to the visual familiarity.

Contrary to the familiarity of the trees was the surprise of massive clumps of bamboo — a common component of this Asian forest community and the dietary staple of the giant panda. The panda is the reason my colleagues brought me here to the Wanglang National Nature Reserve, at the eastern edge of the Tibetan Plateau. I was curious to know this environment, the creatures who lived here, and the scientists who studied them. My feelings of joy at being here were also accompanied by a sense of relief. The previous day's ten-hour highway journey across the Sichuan Basin had presented me a discouraging and perplexing picture of an intensively used and abused agricultural and industrial landscape — a place that held a massive swarm of hard-working people doing all they could to sustain their livelihood.

I had begun my mid-May trip by flying from Seattle to Chengdu, capital city of Sichuan Province, where I was a guest at Sichuan University. I met students and conducted a workshop on applying genetics to analyzing geographic variation of animal populations. The students impressed me with their enthusiasm and curiosity, their many questions, and their ambitions and idealism about the future of their country. I enjoyed my visit to the university, again because of an element of familiarity — the academic world of professors and students and classrooms. From that common platform I was able to appreciate the differences in decorum and culture that showed in the dress, the mannerisms, the

food, and everything else in Asian culture that contrasts
with North America.

I anticipated that getting out into nature would be a
highlight. After several days in Chengdu I was ready to
escape the urban core of Sichuan, with its concentration of
some 15 million people. Asia was a new continent and a new
biotic realm for me, and I was eager to meet new mountains
and forests. In the company of three colleagues from the
university and the provincial wildlife department, we set off
together in the morning in a small van, operated by a
professional driver, heading westward across the flats of the
agriculture-dominated Chengdu Basin. I was the only non-
Chinese in the vehicle, and I enjoyed the process of getting
acquainted with my fellow-scientist hosts, with whom I
quickly felt a sense of professional kinship. I understood
none of the conversation unless it was directed to me, the
guest, in English. Many of my questions in the first part of
the day were about the agricultural countryside and the
busy activities of farmers at the roadside.

All across the Chengdu Basin the mid-May air lay
hot and heavy with dirty gray smoke and haze. The lack of
blue in the sky became more and more discouraging to my
eyes as I watched more and more of the passing landscape.
The smoke and haze—arising from agricultural, domestic,
and industrial activities—produced a tedious and
unpleasant odor and physical irritation as it moved in and
out of my nose and lungs. Uncountable numbers of Chinese
people labored, tilled, and harvested as we flew past them
and I stared from my position in the comfortable front seat.
People of all ages toiled on small plots of wheat, corn, rice,
and green vegetables. Compared to the numbers of people
and dwellings, I saw few cattle, sheep, and goats.

I was surprised that mid spring was already yielding
so much food, and that the tired and hard-working land
itself seemed to be at the end of harvest. Orange tongues of
fire licked at the land everywhere to consume straw,
cornstalks, and other remnants of primary productivity, the

end, my friends explained, of the first harvests of wheat and corn. My colleagues told me that the burning was not allowed, but the people did it anyway, out of desperation and the haste to replant the tired land—more heavy smoke rising to fill the already dirty gray air. I was witnessing continuous work, continuous people, continuous exploitation of Earth, all driven by the needs of many people to eat and to survive. Workers held modest shocks of short-stemmed wheat in their bare hands and threshed them against small boards to collect the grain on small plastic sheets. The work in rice paddies, now being replanted, seemed to represent a life that has gone on forever in this land. Seeing the harvest gave me the secure sense that people were eating, despite all the distressed conditions that I observed across the land. In addition to the agricultural landscape with its rural dwellings and out-buildings, we occasionally crossed small urban centers.

We stopped in a small town for lunch at an open-air restaurant. Dozens of tables covered a raw concrete floor beneath a flat roof cover that shielded us from the sun's heat. The host looked at me and smiled, bowing and nodding in a way that seemed to acknowledge that I was the only person in the establishment who was not of Asian ethnic origin. He proudly walked over to a sound system, popped in a cassette tape, turned it on loudly, and smiled again, in a sort of salute to me, as English-language Christmas carols boomed out from the speakers for all to hear. We ate heartily and well, in family style from large bowls with a selection of vegetables, meat, rice, and noodles.

Later in the afternoon we left the oppressive air and overworked agricultural lowlands behind us, as we drove out of the western edge of the basin. I wondered about the historical stages by which the Chinese culture and economy had transformed the landscape now behind us into such an intense monoculture of humanity. In millennia past, before population growth intensified, this basin must have enjoyed a modest human imprint, probably a more pastoral landscape and more gently cultivated plots of land. The bleak face of the twenty-first-century Chengdu Basin represented to me a tired and highly altered environment that resulted from extensive habitat destruction and environmental degradation. The destruction of the lower elevation forests where pandas formerly lived in recent millennia was only part of that degradation.

I felt some relief from the unpleasant lowlands as I began to see open stands of natural shrub vegetation on rocky ground as we climbed into the foothills of mountains that lay further ahead of us in the distance. It was a quieter place, less busied by human presence. The landscape became more rugged as we arrived in Pingwu County, a large area with less than 200,000 inhabitants, low density for China. We were entering the Minshan Mountains, part of the bigger Hengduan Mountains region. This transitional zone, in western Sichuan Province, rises to the grand Tibetan Plateau. The local native people, the Baima, are of Tibetan ethnic origin, and we passed through their villages of solid, wooden, mountain houses. Ruddy-cheeked villagers were heavily dressed in colorful traditional clothing and wool felt hats, some with a white chicken-feather adornment. Herders stood near their animals out in the scrub vegetation. We began to see natural grass expanses among the bushes, and gradually here and there a few small trees. Goats, sheep, pigs, cattle, and yaks out on the land and in the small village settlements demonstrated the rich array of livestock that these people maintained. My friends told me that the area receives consistent standing snow in winter and has a much reduced growing season for the crops they can produce here: barley, buckwheat, potatoes, and corn.

In early evening the sun had already set by the time we drove into headquarters of the Wanglang National

Nature Reserve, at an elevation just over 8,500 feet, but daylight was still hanging on to show off the surrounding mountain peaks in the soft glow of the early twilight sky. I was sensing the presence of nature for real now, as earlier I had only hoped for it. We stopped at the cluster of simple, attractive buildings consisting of the scientific station, an ecotourism lodge, and other smaller accommodations. On one building I spotted the famous icon of the World Wildlife Fund — thick, black WWF letters and the contrasting black and white elements that form the image of a giant panda, looking at you as it walks forward innocently, curiously, and magnificently. China's black and white bear has come to represent all of Earth's animals and their habitats, which deserve our attention and protection.

The sky darkened as we settled into the lodge, and I checked into my small, cold but comfortably appointed room. The bed was covered with thick blankets. I found the dining room and joined my friends for dinner at a big round table set for eight — our group of five plus the station's director and two wildlife biologists. A warm fire was burning in the fireplace nearby. Servers gradually placed about 15 large bowls of food on our table, from which we helped ourselves to an extensive and tasty array of meats and vegetables, a feast of Sichuan's cuisine as far as I could tell. I was surprised by the different cuts of pork and beef, thick chunks or thin slices, and the variety of novel sauces. My chopstick skills were seriously tested, especially when it came to the tiny roasted peanuts in a slippery sauce. A group of English-speaking tourists, from the UK as I detected by their accents, were seated at a table near ours eating European-style food plates.

Conversation in English at our table, where I remained the only native speaker of English, focused on orientation to the reserve and to the giant panda population here. I had plenty of questions. All of my Chinese colleagues had anecdotes to share about their own experiences at the Wanglang Reserve and with panda research in general. We moved on to talk about the history of giant panda populations and their plight in modern China.

Already by mid-twentieth century only about 3,000 giant pandas remained in Asia, a reduction from much greater numbers that existed before human populations began to occupy and convert earlier forested landscapes into agriculture. A great deal of lowland bamboo, the principal food of pandas, was destroyed in areas that used to support panda populations, and now we know pandas only from the highlands, at elevations from about 5,000 to 10,000 feet. In the 1970s and 80s alone, nearly half of Sichuan's panda habitat was destroyed by deforestation. After the end of the last Pleistocene glaciation, about 15,000 years ago, fossil records tell us that the modern species of giant panda (*Ailuropoda melanoleuca*) lived not only across a broader range in China, but also in Laos, Myanmar, Thailand, and Vietnam. In 2017 we know pandas only from western China, consisting of about 30 isolated populations in high-elevation forests in Sichuan Province and two contiguous provinces to the north. The current population estimate is somewhat below 2,000. Remaining challenges to their conservation, even with protected status and containment in reserves, are timber harvesting, livestock grazing, road construction, and poaching. The key to the conservation plan is of course habitat protection, and the model of the giant panda story has famously made the panda into the symbol of seeking sustainability of animal populations in a human-dominated world.

The story of the giant panda's reduction in numbers and geographic range is also directly symbolic of many other animal species that have declined in response to the expansion of human populations on Earth. Humans have carried out their historical population expansion, along with geographic range expansion, to promote their own survival. The human story is extreme and all the more remarkable when we realize that it started with modest expansions out of Africa, to Asia, to Europe, to Australia, and to the

Americas. The numerical and geographic success of the human species since the age of exploration and the industrial revolution has covered Earth in a most disproportionate way that has completely changed the perspective of our place in nature.

As dinner conversation waned and we prepared to retire for the night in anticipation of our morning hike, conversation from the nearby table caught my attention. One curious voice stood out with an Australian accent. To my surprise, I realized not only that the voice was Australian but that it was the voice of a friend and colleague who had stayed in my lab in Seattle in the past, and whom I had visited in Australia when I lived there for a year. I walked over and shook hands, and I spent a few minutes chatting with him and the tourist group he was hosting as part of a plan to accredit the Wanglang lodge as an ecotourism destination for UK visitors. These kinds of "small-world" encounters don't really end up being all that rare, and they remind us that we really are all connected together on this planet.

I couldn't resist stepping out into the chilly early-morning mountain air for a walk before breakfast, and I was attracted to the river just below the lodge. Mists rose up and water splashed noisily as the river cascaded over boulders and into pools lined with smaller cobbles. I stood and stared at the river and listened to its rushing sounds. Birch trees lined the banks, and flowering rhododendrons and azaleas attracted my attention. I was not acquainted with the small herbs among the grasses at my feet on the frosty ground. The light morning breeze was invigorating, and I walked briskly back to the lodge to meet my friends.

After breakfast we gathered our belongings and a packed lunch to prepare for a day out in the surrounding forest, and we climbed into our van for a short drive to the first trailhead. My friends were not surprised that I asked again about the likelihood of our seeing a panda, and the field station's wildlife biologists who accompanied us were frank in their assurance that it was highly unlikely. Field biologists have demonstrated the solitary, asocial behavior of giant pandas. They are not considered to be particularly wary of humans, but simply do not encounter them because of their continuous, solo wandering through rough mountainous terrain. Even mating and courtship do not involve much social connection or bond, as the female comes into estrus for only one to three days a year, and otherwise has no enduring interest in any male. Adding to this behavioral characterization, the extremely low population density of pandas adds up to the result that not many people ever get to see pandas in the wild, including the biologists who try to study them.

As we followed the trail into a tall forest of dense timber at the base of a rising mountainside, I generally followed along in the middle of our file, so I could talk to any of the colleagues closest to me on either side. The local wildlifers told us that most of the snow had melted away a month ago, in April, from where we were walking. The earliest rhododendrons and azaleas were in flower, and the larch (the unusual, deciduous conifer) had already leafed out fairly well. With our emphasis on observing core panda habitat, we would be sticking to the lower elevations within the reserve, which otherwise extended upward to an alpine zone of shrubs and meadow, at 11,500 to 14,500 feet, and beyond that higher yet to permanent snow fields all the way up to 16,000 feet. Pandas don't roam, at any season, much above 10,000 feet. The panda forests where we walked were a typical temperate-zone mixed-coniferous forest, mainly fir and spruce, with deciduous elements such as birch and poplar.

As with any curious group of scientists, we were all peering into the forest, close and far, uphill and down, looking, sometimes with binoculars, at all the usual and hoping for anything not so usual, such as a panda. Bamboo was aplenty here and there, according to soils and water drainage, and it was more luxuriant where light penetrated more freely down through the canopy of giant old fir and spruce above us. As we approached bamboo clumps, we stopped to touch and examine the blades and stalks (culms) of the bamboo to feel their coarseness, and talk about the parts favored by pandas, including the prize of new young shoots down at ground level.

It was already midmorning, and so we heard few bird songs and calls and saw only a few small birds moving in the taller shrubs near the trail. We walked along into a low, flat place with dark-colored, moist soil, rich in humus and spotted here and there with mushrooms that testified to the quality of a healthy forest floor and the availability of nutrients associated with ongoing decomposition of needles and leaf litter. Bamboo grew here as well, in the more open spaces.

I found myself momentarily at the front of our group as we advanced along the trail. Suddenly, against the darkness of the forest floor, I spotted something just to the side of the trail that seemed almost to glow because of its yellowish tones, though overall it was yellowish-green — a big blob lying there in sharp contrast to the dark-brown, blackish soil, and in the shape and size of an abnormally large baked potato. I immediately knew what it was and crouched down to slide my fingers beneath the strange object — the single dropping of a giant panda!

I stood up and held the astonishing pellet in both hands, extending it admiringly to my colleagues. It was fresh and moist, but well formed and firm due to all the large pieces of tough material that made it up. Taking a pinch out of the pellet in my fingers and rubbing them together, I inhaled a lively and, to me as a biologist, fragrant smell. In turn, we each assisted in plucking the fibrous fecal formation apart, running our fingers through the bamboo bits. We know that if you put bamboo into a panda's mouth, what comes out the other end reflects a digestive extraction of nutrients and energy amounting to only about 20% of the matter contained in the original bite. This means that the pellet I held represented a full 80% of what the panda ate in the first place. No wonder it looked like fresh pieces of bamboo, and no wonder the panda has to eat so much bamboo just to get enough energy to survive. This is a generous form of recycling. Take a little, and put back most of what you took. Panda droppings contribute to the natural humus that develops over time from the decay of their feces and other organic matter on the forest floor here. Pandas have done this for a long time, and the humus they've generated in old forests is only part of their legacy. Take a little, and put back the rest!

One of my Chinese colleagues knew how to decipher the length of the chopped-up bamboo fragments in feces and had developed an equation to predict the approximate body size and age of giant pandas that deposit the various fecal souvenirs that one can collect from the forest here. Depending on the size of the individuals and quality of the bamboo they were eating, pandas could produce from 100 to 170 fecal pellets a day, another of my colleagues pointed out. Pandas regularly make these deposits as they amble along alone through the forest making successive brief encounters with patches of bamboo. Finding each additional clump of bamboo, they munch more luscious bites of shoots, leaves, or stems. They may rest, but again move on, making daily rounds through their home range. This makes up the solitary panda life of searching, eating, resting, and pooping. As a large-sized herbivore (the biggest males nearly 300 pounds) with little concern for enemies, the panda would have no advantage to forming a social feeding group.

Bamboo, despite its tree-like height and stout, hefty canes or stalks, is a member of the grass family, not only the biggest grass, but one of the fastest growing of all plants. This makes bamboo, in its own right, a giant, just as it serves in turn as the culinary favorite of the giant panda. One of the Chinese ecologists with the Sichuan Provincial Department of Forestry pointed to a big footprint, about eight inches long, in some nearby loose soil. Another colleague had recently estimated, by counting the total number of fresh droppings in the area, that perhaps no more than 20 individual giant pandas made up the population here in Wanglang. (Within five years of my visit, a method for measuring DNA in fecal pellets was used to count the number of individuals, with a more encouraging estimate of 66 pandas in Wanglang.)

Although the hope of my visit was naturally to see a panda, that was not to happen, and I had to accept the happy experience of being convinced of their secretive existence by the evidence of fresh dung—first one pellet and then more as we walked on. Although the sum total of my own field observations of the panda in China was a resounding zero, I was able to supplement this modestly when I visited a captive breeding site for pandas back in Chengdu, where I was charmed by the gentle demeanor of pandas lounging about their enclosures munching peacefully on piles and piles of bamboos that were being hauled into their compound.

The story of the evolution of the giant panda is that of a remarkable departure from the meat-eating traditions of the mammalian order Carnivora. To begin with, going back tens of millions of years into the Miocene epoch, pandas have belonged to the bear family (Ursidae), which among all the carnivores already represents adoption of an omnivorous diet of fruits, vegetable material, and a gentle mix of insect and small animal foods, including fish and aquatic organisms. The distinction of the giant panda, among its bear-family kin, is that it evolved into pure grass-eating herbivory beginning as long as 7 to 8 million years ago, with the earliest fossil ancestor of the modern giant panda. The modern genus and species are apparently about 2.5 to 3 million years old, as evidenced from fossils in southern China. The broad, flat grinding teeth and powerful jaws (and a lack of the killer teeth of meat-eating predators) are characteristic of the giant panda, who does formidable work with its jaws and teeth to grind up the huge batches of bamboo that it has to eat every day.

The gut of the giant panda is what really limits its efficiency for extracting energy and nutrition from bamboo. If only the panda had the large, complex, fermenting-chamber guts of antelopes, goats, deer and the other two-hoofed ruminants, or the big stomach and cecum of the zebras and horses and other one-hoofed mammals. But alas, the panda is a giant herbivore trapped in the body of the carnivoran mammal lineage and thus possessing only a small and simple stomach and no cecum—no extra space to hold plant material for a while so it can ferment, which means to allow bacteria and protozoans (the inner microbiome) to do the digesting for them. Thus pandas have little or no fermentation going on in their gut. The end game is just extreme inefficiency of nutrient extraction coupled with an extremely rapid rate of passing everything through the simple, short gut. That's why panda poo doesn't look or smell much different from the bamboo they eat in the first place.

The panda does have a stunning evolutionary modification of its hand, in fact the enlargement of the first of the wrist bones. This hand bone, operated by a powerful muscle, is moved forcefully, like a giant thumb, to hold and strip bamboo stems (culms) of their leaves so that the panda can ingest a greater proportion of the nutrient-rich leafy material, after which they may chew and crack the tough culms with their teeth, if they bother to eat them at all.

Most recently the understanding that the Chinese are obtaining of giant panda behavior and population biology is improving because they can place GPS collars on the animals out in nature to record daily movement activity. This helps to make up for the fact that in the past only a few direct observations of panda movements and activities in the wild had ever been made. The new results show that giant panda activity seems to be concentrated in a morning period, a later afternoon period, and then, surprisingly, still more activity in the middle of the night. This is consistent with the idea that they should require many hours of daily foraging activity to keep enough food moving, inefficiently as it does, through their guts.

The beauty of western Sichuan's rugged mountains, the pristine forests of the Wanglang National Nature Reserve, and the remarkable evolutionary history of the unusual herbivore trapped in the body of a carnivore all hold me in awe of the giant panda. It was a joy to experience how all of this has come together on the Asian continent, making for me a most memorable trip to China.

Why do we have an enthusiastic emotional response toward the large black and white bear known as the giant panda? Most humans have positive emotional responses toward at least some kinds of animals, even big ones. The panda is high up on many lists, even though few people, including me, may ever see a panda in the wild. People experience animals and nature in a variety of different ways. Some love to connect with smaller creatures such as the birds they can lure into their gardens, patios, or balconies with food, creating a satisfying personal connection with nature. Although that connection occurs on the terms and in the personal living space of people, it works for satisfying a longing to be connected with the creatures that otherwise inhabit natural spaces.

What does the voice of the giant panda tell us now? What did I hear it say as I walked around with dedicated Chinese colleagues in the forests of Wanglang National Nature Reserve? And what did it say as we examined the large fresh fecal pellet on the forest floor that revealed so much to me about the complexity of giant panda life? Can we direct our much-needed attention to solving the big problems looming at the global scale of climate change and habitat loss? The big-scale problems require big-scale attention. We must find actions that assure Earth's survival, and for that the survival of healthy habitats and species. Our place in nature is no longer that of nomadic hunters or sedentary agriculturists, isolated by distance from one another and living in occasional pockets of land here and there. Earth is now covered with humanity, and the rare pockets of today are the diminishing number of small areas that appear to be free of human exploitation and interference. We must seek now to stabilize and eventually to reverse the unintended outcomes of our rampant domination of Earth. I have recently, in 2017, been encouraged to see that the Chinese are acknowledging the realities of climate change and the value of adopting green policies. I believe we can find solutions, and I believe that our understanding of the beauty of nature can motivate us to that positive goal.

12

GROUND SQUIRREL
WHO ATE CHIPMUNKS

The summer warmth, blue skies, and smell of ponderosa pine attracted me first as a youngster and always welcomed me back to what I think of as my favorite mountain habitat, on the dry east side of the Cascade Mountains. My first memories of this forest were in my childhood, in Oregon, and I returned to the ponderosa in my adult life, in Washington. The iconic animal inhabitant of these woods, for me, was the golden-mantled ground squirrel, the little charmer who always showed up in campgrounds and on picnic tables, quite willing to risk exposure in exchange for any little food scrap, or perhaps a peanut. One morning my father cut open a cantaloupe on an old wooden forest-service table and spooned out the melon's innards onto the tabletop, whereupon the resident "goldie" boldly jumped up to the bench and then to the table top to enjoy the juicy pile of seeds and stringy stuff resting at the far end of the table while we watched with delight and ate traditional melon slices off our plates.

Washes of copper and gold around the shoulders, neck, and snout are the signature ID of the golden-mantled ground squirrel that seem to reflect the warmth and attraction this creature holds for humans who visit where it lives. The black and white stripes on its back lead many to believe this animal is a chipmunk, but chipmunks — spry and much smaller members of the squirrel family — have stripes on their faces as well, while golden mantels have a plain face. I always felt I saw eye to eye with the golden mantle, more personally than with other animals, and perhaps that's because the golden mantle's dark eyes are surrounded by a lovely whitish ring. It must've been the eye ring that captured my attention and assured me that the golden-mantled ground squirrel was looking back at me.

My father helped me catch a golden-mantled ground squirrel that I kept as a pet for several years in a large outdoor cage. That was how I first learned about the ground squirrel's annual cycle: getting big and fat by summer's end, disappearing completely for the autumn and winter into the nest box filled with old cloth rags shredded for insulation, and surprising me that it was still alive when I found the stuffing mysteriously missing from the nest box doorway the following spring. Joyously for me, the creature reappeared to reacquaint itself with its cage and announce the arrival of spring by hopping onto the big running wheel to take the first vigorous strides of the new year. It was later no surprise that this animal became the object of many years of research during my professional career.

The setting of my decade-long ecological study on a population of golden-mantled ground squirrels in the 1980s and 90s was an intermediate elevation forest on the east side of Washington's north Cascades, at about 2,000 feet elevation, located midway between a mountain pass and the lowlands of the Columbia Plateau. The open landscape of the mixed ponderosa pine and Douglas-fir forest was a contrast to western Washington's denser, wetter forests. The handsome ponderosas, with long, dark green needles set three in each fascicle and with trunks of older trees showing deep furrows of dark color alternating with orange and light brown superficial bark, occupied only these intermediate and lower elevations, thinning out to the east into the upper-most stands of sagebrush. I always liked the flakey texture of the bark, with its layers of jig-saw-puzzle pieces, and the big cones scattered on the ground were always irresistible to pick up, hold, and then toss back onto the carpet of old dry needles covering the forest floor.

The golden-mantled ground squirrel of Washington's Cascade Mountains and neighboring southern British Columbia is known as *Callospermophilus saturatus*, which is different from the species I got to know as a youngster in the Oregon Cascades, *Callospermophilus lateralis*. The *lateralis* species is better known because it covers a broad range across western North America from Oregon southward into California's Sierra Nevada and across the intermountain west and the entire Rocky Mountain chain up into southern Canada. Perhaps some geographic isolating event during ice-age glacial cycles of the Pleistocene Epoch divided off the populations now in Washington and British Columbia where they consolidated their identity as *saturatus*. As far as ground squirrel aficionados are concerned, the two species pretty much share the same ecology and behavior.

In 1986 we were in the second year of our intense study of the population of golden mantles living in our study area of about 50 acres—a rectangle measuring about two-tenths by four-tenths of a mile on a side. Our emphasis was on the reproductive efforts of females from the time of mating, in early April, through pregnancy and then nearly five weeks of nursing their young before the pups emerged onto the surface in mid June. The team, usually five of us, was composed of undergraduate assistants, a technician, a postdoc, and myself. In April, May, and June we worked on the study grid for a total of 71 days, with only 20 days off. This was a busy time for mother ground squirrels, and that meant it was a busy time for us monitoring the status and condition of all the marked individuals in our area on a nearly daily basis.

During the first few hours of each morning three of us trapped, examined, weighed, and released the animals, who repeatedly returned to our traps for the modest bait rewards we offered. Whichever team members were not trapping first thing in the morning could begin by observing specific individual squirrels. The rest of us generally spent the remainder of the day walking around following individuals to record their behavior or trying to locate the secret hole in the ground that was the home burrow of each mother and her litter of three to five pups that would eventually emerge from the burrow. We left our 276 traps permanently in place (and usually closed) throughout the whole field season; the grid consisted of rows and columns about 100 feet apart. This routine was similar to what a lot of other field biologists were doing in those same years to investigate populations of small mammals. And meanwhile other researchers were doing similar studies with birds, lizards, frogs, or other critters.

We had spent some earlier days observing our site and setting out the traps in mid March, which also served to demonstrate that the squirrels were still below ground, hibernating, because we saw no signs of them. The ground was still partially covered with the snow that had blanketed the entire south-facing hillside of our study area throughout the winter. We were ready to detect the end of hibernation and the appearance of the first squirrels above ground.

As the snow melted, approaching the end of March, small herbs sprouted and began to grow, forming the first salad greens that would nourish the squirrels and supply their water needs when they emerged from their hibernation burrows. Groundsel was the most abundant herb and the early season favorite of our squirrels, but yarrow and vetch added to the diversity of the salad bowl. Golden mantles and other ground squirrel species in general are well known to be fundamentally herbivorous, or vegetarian as we say.

In our first season, the previous year, we had visually documented (with many hours of sit-and-watch binocular observation) 753 feeding episodes by ground squirrels, often lasting ten minutes or more each, and from this we found that 80% of all the items eaten in the early months of spring were the leaves of small herbs. Over the entire active season, reaching into the dry and hot summer, after the herbs had flowered and dried up, the diet progressively shifted to more and more truffles, which are basically underground mushrooms. The ground squirrels enthusiastically sniffed out, dug up, and consumed the moist flesh of the truffles, which became 60% of the total monthly diet by July and August.

Of many reasons that I admire golden mantles, their consumption of truffles is high on the list, because it sets them apart from many other common rodents and aligns them, in my view, with the sophistication of French cuisine. Other than greens and truffles, only a small fraction of the golden-mantle diet was comprised of other items such as grasses and seeds, and we never observed our squirrels eating insects.

The first male golden-mantled ground squirrels appeared on the surface in late March, running around in search of females, which they did not find. The season began with males only, who were already turned on sexually under physiological controls in the brain that prepared them on an internally driven calendar to start courting and mating as soon as they came above ground and managed to encounter the first females that emerged and went into heat (estrus). By early April the first females were coming out of their burrows and mating with the patrolling males. By early May the females were giving birth, and it was all we could do to keep up with the observations and trapping records to document the days on which each one gave birth (signaled by a drop in body weight and open condition of the birth canal), after which they showed signs of extended nipples and visually conspicuous milk in the mammary tissue.

I had returned to Seattle for a few days of responsibilities at the university and with my family. But I kept in touch with the crew, reaching them via a phone booth at a small country store a few miles from our remote study site and near the old cabin on a small lake where we stayed. It was time for me to return and join the action, and we were pleased that all the routines for data collection and behavioral observation were working well.

The phone call I got on the day before I returned included a bizarre report, and I made the two-hour drive from Seattle over to the study area eagerly waiting to hear the first-hand accounts of what the crew had actually seen. At the end of the day on May 19, when everyone jumped into the van to head back to the cabin, they stopped abruptly just a short distance down the dusty dirt track to check out a squirrel standing on top of an old stump about 25 feet off to the side of road.

It was female 55, recognized by a unique wedge-shaped bleach mark we had placed on her rump fur—the simple way we and other researchers used for field ID of individual ground squirrels or other small mammals at the time. Sitting upright, she was holding the limp body of a chipmunk, with the carcass dangling downward so that the tail and hind feet of the chipmunk rested at the feet of the ground squirrel. Missing from a bloody spot between the shoulders was the chipmunk's head. With the windows rolled down and everyone's binoculars trained on the weird event, the crew watched in awe as 55 proceeded to bite off, chew, and swallow the shoulders, arms, paws, fur, and onward through the torso and internal organs until at least half of the chipmunk was consumed. The ground squirrel was undistracted by the stopped van and observers, but of course our squirrels were accustomed to our routine presence at comfortable short distances.

After 12 minutes of this shocking performance, duly recorded on a sheet in our our observation log, the squirrel lowered herself to a four-leg walking position and descended from the stump with the remaining half of the chipmunk carcass firmly held in her mouth. She released the chipmunk's body, dug a hole in loose soil, placed the carcass in the hole, and covered it. She ran a short distance toward her nearby home burrow, where her eighteen-day-old pups were waiting, safely below in their nest. She paused to nibble on some greens. Was this the salad course after the meat? She dashed over and entered her burrow to join her young. It was the end of her day on the surface. Female 55 was a yearling, whom we'd captured for the first time as a youngster the previous June. She had grown up over the course of the summer and was captured regularly up through September 25, after which she hibernated until the beginning of April of the following year. To this point in her life and ours, she had been just another squirrel on the grid. The crew could only sit, spellbound, in the van for a few more minutes, remarking repeatedly and animatedly to one another about what they had just witnessed. This was over-the-top unusual. It didn't match anything we had ever seen before. A ground squirrel eating a chipmunk? Hadn't we just last season documented the full and exclusive, peaceful vegetarian life style of all the squirrels in our population?

In collecting my thoughts based on anything I'd ever read, I recalled published reports of cannibalism in ground squirrels, which amounted to sightings of ground squirrels eating road-kill of their own kind. Also the killing of juvenile ground squirrels by non-kin (infanticide) had been reported for several species, but that behavior was related to social competition and did not involve eating the dead squirrels. In any event, it was known that ground squirrels could kill other small mammals and that they have been observed eating them on rare occasions. We were surprised by the unusual behavior we had observed in one individual in our population, and we wanted to respond to our collective curiosity by trying to find out what was really going on with female 55. We wondered how she had obtained the chipmunk carcass.

The delightful little chipmunks living in great numbers on our study area were yellow-pine chipmunks, *Tamias amoenus*, named after the ponderosa pine, and commonly associated with both ponderosas and golden-mantled ground squirrels, all as members of the same ecological community living in the western United States and Canada. Weighing just 2 ounces, the adult chipmunks were only about one-fourth the size of a golden mantle. The ground squirrel should be able to subdue the chipmunk rather handily, but the bigger challenge for the ground squirrel would be to catch the frisky-frenetic chipmunk in the first place.

We decided to put one of our crew, Suzanne, on special assignment for the next day to follow female 55's every move. Everyone else would manage all the routine trapping and observing required for May 20. Suzanne was good at spending long periods of time tracking, and importantly not losing, individual squirrels, as she recorded their minute-by-minute, all-day-long activities in various categories that we designated in our protocol: walking, running, feeding, sitting, etc. (We had good ways to provide break times and relief by having other crew members stand in while any observer took a needed break now and then during such day-long observation duties.) Beyond Suzanne's expertise, she enjoyed the work and found it satisfying, as did many other students who signed on as field assistants over the years. We were all excited to find out further clues to place the previous day's observation in a bigger context.

Because we knew the location of 55's maternal burrow, Suzanne was able to station herself near the entrance hole and wait for the squirrel to emerge, which she did at 6:40 a.m. Her first move was a bee-line to the site where she had buried the half carcass at the end of the previous day. She unearthed the carcass and proceeded to bite off, chew, and swallow nearly all the rest of the bits and pieces, leaving only a fragment of the tail and a small wad of fur. The rest of 55's morning was occupied with typical behavior, mostly digging and eating truffles, and twice going for some greens. When another squirrel passed near 55's home burrow, she chased it away. By mid morning she went underground and did not return to the surface for four hours, typical of the usual midday break from the surface taken by lactating mothers in our population. This was a major block of time for the mother to care for her young, keep them warm, and provide her rich milk for their nutrition.

Throughout the entire day 55 had no associations with any of the active chipmunks that moved around frequently in her area. They seemed to pay one another no heed. Her only interactions with other animals on the surface that day were several chase-offs of intruding fellow ground squirrels in defense of her home foraging area. The chasing behavior was typical for golden-mantled ground squirrels, which are considered to be an asocial species. During the afternoon 55 fed again largely on truffles but included occasional bits of green food.

Near the end of her long day, Suzanne was rewarded with one observation that reinforced what happened the day before. In the late afternoon 55 walked around to a different part of her home area, dug into the soil and pulled out another carcass. This was yet another half-chipmunk, the rear half. We could assume that she had, on some previous day (and not today) probably eaten the front half of this animal, as she was able to recognize the present site and uncover its contents. She proceeded, as before, to bite off, chew, and swallow the bits of the rear half of the chipmunk carcass she had just uncovered. She left the tail, which Suzanne later picked up as a souvenir. Female 55 continued to rove around her usual feeding places for the rest of the afternoon, consumed more truffles and greens, and at 5:17

p.m. she retired, in the usual way, into her burrow to spend the night nursing and caring for her young.

We had our hands full with routine monitoring of all the lactating mothers in our population, but we kept our eyes on female 55 incidentally and we captured and examined her four times in the next ten days. We expected that her young would be emerging in about two weeks. On May 31 we decided to have Suzanne follow her again for the day.

Female 55 emerged from her burrow at 5:40 a.m., earlier than she had 11 days before and matching the lengthening of daylight, with the solstice now only three weeks ahead. After digging up a truffle that she ate immediately, she moved into a thicket of snowbrush ceanothus (*Ceanothus velutinus*), the most common shrub in the understory of our forest. These aromatic evergreen shrubs, mostly three to five feet tall and with shiny green oval-shaped leaves on slender flexible branches, formed dense tangles of cover into which ground squirrels and chipmunks would often dive. When they did that, we would momentarily lose sight of them, though we could hear them rummaging around in the litter of the thicket. When female 55 emerged a couple of minutes later she was carrying the bottom half of a chipmunk! Sitting near the edge of the ceanothus, she spent 13 minutes eating most of the carcass and then buried the small amount of leftovers. She moved out, found another truffle, and walked a short distance to bury it, perhaps already feeling sated with her most recent meaty meal.

She continued moving slowly toward another ceanothus thicket where a chipmunk was sitting. As 55 approached the chipmunk, she suddenly jumped at it, and both of them scrambled into the ceanothus tangle for an ensuing noisy skirmish, with dry leaves rattling. Momentarily the chipmunk shot out of the brush and ran away. A miss for 55!

This was our first observation of an attempted

predation by a golden-mantled ground squirrel on a chipmunk. Though the ground squirrel was unsuccessful, it showed us at least what female 55 was doing, and probably pretty often, given now our several observations of her eating chipmunks. We had to continue. We wanted to see the ultimate event, the kill. How did the ground squirrel do it? But in the next hour Suzanne observed female 55 switching to another activity—nest-building. She made 15 trips into a different burrow from the one currently holding her pups, on each trip carrying grasses and other plant material. We observed this behavior often, and had learned that mother golden mantles frequently established new nests in nearby alternative burrows. They subsequently took advantage of these other sites, most often following a predatory threat by a long-tailed weasel. Once a vigilant mother chased off the weasel or otherwise avoided it, her next line of defense, after the weasel's departure, was to mouth-carry each of her young, one per trip, to the awaiting new burrow. After female 55 completed her nest-building work (in this case an investment for a future emergency) she showed Suzanne she was ready for a meaty snack. At 8:26 a.m. she returned to where she had buried the remainders of the chipmunk she was eating earlier, and she uncovered it and ate up all the rest. The remainder of female 55's day continued rather routinely, with no other behaviors related to chipmunk hunting or eating.

Two days later, on June 2, Suzanne again shadowed female 55. It turned out to be a remarkable day of dramatic predation attempts—five separate attacks on chipmunks, but unfortunately none of them successful. It was revealing to see how frequent and regular 55's attempts were, but frustrating not to observe a successful kill. Suzanne was the most disappointed because she had invested so much time. The first attack was at 6:19 a.m., and two baby chipmunks— potentially easier to snatch than adults—were the targets. Quick and agile, the babies ran up a small ponderosa pine, and the ground squirrel followed, but only for the first couple of feet up the trunk before she gave up. Ground squirrels, after all, belong on the ground, not in trees. I once observed a juvenile ground squirrel that climbed slowly up a young ponderosa pine with slender flexible lower branches; the little ground squirrel may have entered the tree in response to my presence. What else to do? It crawled out toward the tip of a branch that began to droop downward, with the comical result (funny to me) that it fell out of the tree, and ran away.

Female 55 attempted her second predation of the morning half an hour later as she was moving along the dirt road that wound through our grid. She paused when she spotted two baby chipmunks headed up the road toward her. She waited motionlessly in ambush until they were within a few feet of her and then sprang at them, but missed, as they ran away back down the road. Oddly, she immediately began to gather grass nest material, which on this occasion may have been displacement behavior, in other words doing something out of context following the failed predation. Forty-five minutes later, 55 raced out to chase another chipmunk that ran away from her. Another hour later, at 8:37 a.m., she was walking along a fallen log and spotted a chipmunk feeding on the ground. She crept slowly up to within a couple of feet of the chipmunk and stopped. She lunged at the chipmunk, and it issued a loud squeak of alarm and ran off, with 55 pursuing for only a few feet before giving up. Alarm calls are considered to be useful for the animal giving the call because the announcement tells the predator "I see you, and thus you have less chance to catch me." The alarm call is also an alert to danger for one's own kind nearby. The fifth and final chipmunk chase of the day didn't occur until nearly four o'clock in the afternoon, when 55 was again feeding next to a snowbrush ceanothus, in which a chipmunk also happened to show up for some foraging. The ground squirrel moved in a stalking crawl toward the chipmunk, but the chipmunk saw the ground squirrel, gave an alarm call, and ran off.

Over the next three weeks we sighted female 55 around the grid on seventeen occasions, and we trapped her ten times. Everything seemed to be progressing normally in her life as a mother, and through our remaining brief observations we didn't happen to see any more chipmunk-eating behavior. Her three young emerged from the maternal burrow at the middle of the month, and on June 16, we saw her and her young all together near their burrow. She was calling out to them with the authoritative motherly chirps that presumably guided them to recognize her presence and her vigilance as they began their lives exploring the surface environment that was to become their world. The last time we captured female 55 was June 21. After that, we presumed she must have been lost to one of our local mammal carnivores — weasel, marten, coyote — or maybe a goshawk.

The novelty of female 55's behavior in May and June of 1986 captured our attention and aroused our curiosity as much as anything else we observed in the otherwise routine, common behavior of so many other individuals over a decade at our study site. We found it bizarre, this habit of roving around like a carnivore to kill and eat members of another species. What she did was a testament to the flexibility of the mammalian brain and behavior. Some early event in her life, out foraging for the usual foods must have attracted her attention to a moving chipmunk as something she could attack. Somehow she grabbed and killed it, and ate it, and then subsequently repeated what had worked once. She bit off their heads and consumed the carcasses, certainly many of them. The behavior reinforced itself through success. She developed an expertise that no other golden-mantled ground squirrel in our area was practicing. And certainly no other golden-mantled ground squirrel that anyone else has reported in the scientific literature.

We also know that the success of 55's foraging novelty did not persist within the population. The simplest opportunity for that to occur would have amounted to cultural learning, in other words other ground squirrels, whether her own young or others, could potentially observe and then copy her behavior. Her behavior clearly did not become fixed through natural selection in the population, nor has any such behavior, as far as we know, become fixed in any of the many other species of ground squirrels. We do recognize other cases in evolutionary history where the diet of one species has taken an evolutionary divergence from an initially established pattern within a family or a genus.

The chisel-toothed kangaroo rat, for example, became the only leaf-eating specialist in a genus of about twenty other species of kangaroo rats that feed mostly on seeds. And how about the giant panda, who went the opposite way of our little female 55, from meat to plants! Sometime, perhaps more than five million years ago, a panda ancestor began to abandon the traditions of the carnivoran mammal lineage and of the bear family by scrapping the meat diet and murderous behavior. The panda's change in dietary behavior and modification of its teeth for grinding bamboo were among the permanent, evolutionary changes that converted the giant panda into a bamboo specialist and pure vegetarian. Our two short years of observing the life of female 55 were not enough time for golden-mantled ground squirrels to initiate a new evolutionary trend.

In the modern era, we humans are doing more than we could have imagined a millennium ago to expand and diversify our eating behavior and diet, and our cuisine. Our flexible brain and our regional and global exchanges of culture have taken us down many pathways. We were already equipped, since the early history of *Homo sapiens*, with the teeth and digestive tract of a generalized mammalian omnivore. Our contemporary dietary choices are influenced by vast writings and pop culture that range across nutritional science and pure social fads to the culinary arts. Procurement of food is easy for many, but not all of us, through convenient markets of many kinds.

Those of us in the privileged world sample and enjoy foods that come from every continent and biogeographic realm, even as we strive to grow many of these things locally. We make the further personal choices to remain omnivores, or to be vegetarians or vegans, or to eat junk food. The variable psychological make-up within the human population introduces further diversity and complexity to human eating habits, including the unfortunate dietary patterns that are classified as eating disorders. All in all, what each of us eats becomes a matter of personal whim together with adherence to the constantly changing smorgasbord of nutritional theory, educational dogma, and our sensitivities to environmental issues of where and how food is grown.

Our own species, because of our brains and our culture, seems to move again and again into arenas that go beyond the laws of nature — the good laws that are supposed to govern survival of all the species on Earth. The life of one unusual golden-mantled ground squirrel who ate chipmunks was an intellectual curiosity for me and an amusement that provided an example of what the mammalian brain can do out there in the wilds of nature. Perhaps when we are able to identify and appreciate situations that are unusual or not natural, we gain a better perspective on the reality of nature's way on our Earth.

13

CAUGHT IN THE ACT

COURTSHIP, MATING, AND BIRTH

As I walked quietly in evening twilight over sand and around hillocks on which old, stalwart desert bushes grew, I was startled by two small vigorously struggling animals, locked together, kicking sand, kicking one another, and growling, as best a rodent can growl. I felt like I might have stepped on them, but I hadn't. They were only a few feet away, their long, stout tails swirling in the air and beating the sand. I stopped in my tracks, frozen, to figure out what was going on. I recognized the two creatures as chisel-toothed kangaroo rats, *Dipodomys microps*, both males as I subsequently detected. I was out for evening field work at my dissertation study site in California's Owens Valley. I had just finished setting the little box live-traps on my grid, and the sun had dropped below the crest of the Sierra Nevada about half an hour before I stumbled onto this special *moment in nature*.

After another 15 seconds of rolling around in the flying sand, the two kangaroo rats terminated their locked skirmish, and one of them retreated to a nearby bush. The prevailing male began to survey the sandy hillock from which he had driven off his adversary. As he hopped slowly around, he seemed to pause in stride as he produced a sound I had never heard before: a light drumming with his big hind feet against the sandy surface. I scrambled to grab my clipboard and began scribbling notes. Each pummeling pulse of the drumming lasted only about a second, and within a minute he repeated his drum roll several times as he patrolled over the hillock. I had read previously about "drumming behavior," as reported in laboratory observations of kangaroo rats, but the authors had expressed uncertainty about the function of the behavior, probably because of the contrived and artificial conditions in the laboratory.

The male continued his patrol, with further drumming here and there over the hillock, and then he paused as he approached a two-inch diameter hole, the entrance to an underground burrow. He drummed, as if knocking at the doorstep to the burrow. He circled again and returned to the burrow entrance, drumming. What would happen next? It was a mild March evening at the vernal equinox, and I was witnessing a remarkable behavioral sequence.

He continued to circle around the mound, drumming. He returned again to the burrow entrance. Then it happened. Another kangaroo rat emerged from the hole at which he was drumming. The two bolted at one another, but made no contact and stood in a face-off about six inches apart for a few seconds. Then the new kangaroo rat—I was guessing it was a female—turned and retreated into the hole from which she had just emerged. The male resumed his patrol in a tight loop near the entrance, drumming repeatedly, and in the next moment the other male hopped back onto the scene, arriving at the edge of the female's hillock. As the original male was returning toward the hole, the two charged at one another, leaping a good foot and a half into the air, swirling around, and landing on the ground, whereupon the original male chased the intruder five or six feet away from the female's burrow, where the two locked together in another growling, churning fight that lasted for about 15 seconds, as I checked the moving hand on my wristwatch. Neither male became seriously injured, and I saw no blood. The intruder again turned out to be the loser, as indicated by his rapid flight across the desert floor to a distant bush some 50 feet away. He was apparently out of the picture, for the moment. I had quickly come to distinguish the two males from one another early along by some unique features of their tail fur.

The triumphant male hopped the short distance from the spot of the second fight back to the opening of the female's burrow. Momentarily she re-emerged and moved slowly a few feet away to another hole at the top of her home hillock. He pursued her slowly, and she became motionless a few inches from the second burrow opening. Without further ceremony or contacting gestures, he simply mounted her at this moment and began a continuous series of pelvic thrusting movements that lasted about 45 seconds. It was now clear that the fighting between the two males and the patrolling and drumming to promote contact between male and female were all about obtaining the exclusive rights for one male to prevail as the successful sire of this female's offspring. The male dismounted, and the female took a few unsteady steps to the side and groomed herself with her front paws and mouth for another 10 seconds or so. The male hopped away, abandoning the scene, and moments later the female departed in another direction out across the desert. We were still in the midst of evening twilight, the sun had disappeared below the Sierra crest about an hour before the mating event, and I had been able to observe all of this detail and record it on my clipboard with good visibility in the dimming natural skylight.

A couple of minutes later, as I continued to stand motionlessly, writing notes and collecting my thoughts, another kangaroo rat appeared on the scene. Alas, as I quickly determined, it was the number two male once again, seemingly checking back as if to see what he had missed. Although he had clearly been displaced by the stronger aggressive force of the prevailing male, this guy was being persistent, and why not? Here he was, all alone now, searching over the female's burrow and drumming for the first time (within my observation). In fact only two minutes had passed since the copulation was completed, and upon finding no others in the immediate vicinity he entered one of the female's tunnel openings. He emerged about 30 seconds later and left the area. Within another minute the female returned and entered one of the holes. And within yet another minute the successful male circled back through the area, inspecting the surface above the female's burrow system, but not drumming. He then departed from the area. Clearly I was now observing some quality-control inspection by male number one, and each of the players had apparently made his or her final curtain call. Within another half hour of watching and waiting, and because I observed no further appearances by any members of the local community, I decided to move along to other matters.

On the following night I returned and spent about an hour and a half to check back for any recurring connections between the players of the previous evening. I eventually saw all three of them. The female emerged more than half an hour after sunset. She paused briefly outside her burrow entrance to urinate, leaving a moist spot that I could see in the sand. She hopped away to a nearby saltbush and began foraging on its leaves. Within about 20 minutes the number-two male showed up, drumming as he approached. He hopped up to the burrow entrance and sniffed at the still-wet urine spot, and with that he hopped away. Perhaps he could tell that her condition had changed. Ten minutes later, the successful male of the previous evening showed up. Very popular place! He also sniffed the urine spot, and then seemingly content with the information gained, he hopped away at great speed.

On the third night I repeated the same schedule and saw all three animals again, one at a time, never together, showing me no social interactions or behaviors of the kind I saw on the first night. They simply moved around on their own, foraging. It seems we had returned to business as usual for kangaroo rats, bearing out the solitary behavior that typifies most of the days of a kangaroo rat lifetime.

I had learned some remarkable lessons from a set of incidental observations that just popped out at me on a few otherwise routine nights out on my study area. I was impressed that the kangaroo rats, after all the initial sparring and investigation on the surface by two potential suitors in bright, early twilight, were willing to perform the ultimate consummatory act right out in the open, rather than in a dark underground lair. There I was, just standing as a scientifically minded voyeur in awe and appreciation of the chance to satisfy curiosity. And there was the mating pair, exposed not only to me but to any number of potential predators. What I observed in general was consistent with a well-known aspect of adult kangaroo rat behavior: that they are not socially bonded animals who live together in the same burrow. (No two of them, either male or female, will generally tolerate one another on a sustained basis in a laboratory cage.) Furthermore, with the promiscuous mating system that accompanies the life history of kangaroo rats, the successful male was foot loose and fancy-free to leave the scene of the copulatory act and furthermore to leave the female alone to gestate, lactate, and care for their young through the day of their ultimate dispersal from the natal nest. The male, finished with his brief and transient commitment to the female, was all about maximizing his fitness by hopping off into the neighborhood to inseminate any other estrous female he could find.

In the months that followed, I recaptured these same three individuals that I had observed fighting and mating several times, and I confirmed their ongoing reproductive condition. The males continued through the waning stages of their breeding season and the female advanced through her pregnancy, eventually gave birth, and showed signs of lactation, with active, protruding nipples and conspicuous white, mammary tissue visible through the thin skin of her belly.

I was pleased with the surprise reward I received when I stumbled onto these important events at the kangaroo rat spring equinox. The opportunity for a scientist to catch such acts in progress is rare. As far as the little desert rodents themselves were concerned, mating is something they accomplish, if lucky, only a few times in a lifetime at most, and these rare events last for only a few minutes. What I got to observe on this occasion clearly was not everyday behavior.

We know from a combination of field and laboratory studies that the gestation period of a kangaroo rat is about four weeks. A mother chisel-toothed kangaroo rat typically gives birth to only two or three young. A newborn chisel-tooth weighs only about one-seventh of an ounce, and it nurses from its mother's milk for only about three weeks before it is ready to show up outside the burrow, at which time it weighs nearly one ounce. The typical production by a mother of only two babies results by four weeks after birth in young who weigh together as much as the mother herself. That is rapid growth! If one is doing the math here and comparing to humans, it's obvious that a pair of month-old human twins do not together weigh nearly as much as their mother. It's clear that a lactating mother rodent's relative performance in terms of energy expenditure and production of mass greatly exceeds that of the human mother's production of a single small and slowly growing youngster.

I was surprised one night, back at the university lab some time later, when I entered a dark animal room where I was keeping a group of kangaroo rats, housed individually in tidy little lab cages that were part of a physiological study I was conducting. Ordinarily I would perform my checks of their food and bedding during the daytime, when the automatically controlled lights were on, but on this day I was on a late schedule. I entered the room and interrupted the normal nighttime of the kangaroo rats by abruptly flipping on a switch to override the darkness. Everything was looking normal until I peeked into the top of another one of the cages. A female stood, hunched over, on her two big hind feet, holding a bloody purple disc in her front paws. Beneath her belly, squirming slightly, I saw a tiny pink newborn pup, still a bit of blood on its body. The mother was, I quickly recognized, eating the placenta that had accompanied the youngster out of her womb. This is normal rodent behavior, though I had never witnessed it before. She completed her efficient recycling of the valuable protein tissue by eating the entire placenta. Then she turned her attention to her little one, resting on the sandy cage bottom at her feet. She licked and cleaned it, and tucked it in beneath her.

As I collected my thoughts and waited a few minutes to see if something else was going to happen, the female moved her feet on the floor and arched her back, flexing her head back down toward her feet. She wavered about a bit on her feet and then raised up and bent back down to produce a huge and rather quick expulsion. Within a few seconds another youngster and another placenta emerged in quick succession. The mother was licking and touching everything with her paws. As I wondered about what she would do next, she manipulated the strange living objects at her feet and somehow singled out a cord, the umbilicus, which she bit. She continued touching everything, testing for what all she had to deal with. As she must have done just minutes before I had first entered the room, she again separated the placenta with bites and licks and consumed it. She next turned her attention to the second little one, licking and cleaning. She cleaned herself with her paws and her mouth, licking. She checked both youngsters. Back and forth, testing, touching, licking, sniffing, hands and mouth busy with so much to do—ignoring the strange bright light and the strange scientist standing there above her in awe.

I was feeling shocked and yet privileged to have happened on this amazing moment in the cycle of life. The mother kangaroo rat was performing some behaviors that most female rodents living in nature will only carry out once or twice in an entire lifetime, and the behavioral events themselves will only last a few minutes. And here I was, a witness. I thought of all the innate programs of behavior in which the mother had been engaged in the last fraction of an hour. How did she and her body know what to do? What did the first signals from the uterus mean to the mother as the womb began to contract and produce twitches of what may or may not have been perceived as pain? How did she distinguish the umbilical cord and know to cut it? What led her to eat the placenta? We do not know how all these innate behaviors work. These are barely once-in-a-lifetime events—nothing the mother can practice ahead of time. I was the fortunate observer of these remarkable events that launched the beginning of air-breathing life for two little kangaroo rats. I decided it was time to make a quiet exit. I switched off the lights and left the room.

The surprising observation of the birth of tiny baby kangaroo rats in the lab added unexpectedly to my field experience observing the mating of the male and female chisel-toothed kangaroo rats. Although it didn't happen out in the desert, the laboratory birth was as much a natural event as anything I ever experienced in the field, and the emotional impact of seeing the wonder of new life left me deeply humbled. It was unforgettable nature on top of nature, as if I had actually been a visitor deep underground in the burrow of a mother kangaroo rat out in Owens Valley's shadscale scrub desert.

EPILOGUE

THE FUTURE OF WILD PLACES

It is the naturalist's privilege
to choose almost any kind
of plant or animal for examination...

Edward O. Wilson, 1984, *Biophilia*

It is indeed a privilege and a delight to be a naturalist — to look for any and every plant and animal that presents itself to us when we get out into nature. I believe that anybody who wants to be a naturalist should claim the title. The field is wide open. Anybody can do it. The subject matter is as grand as the full biodiversity of everything living on Earth, not only the panda, the blue whale, the rhino and the gorilla. Not only the giant redwood, the California poppy, the silverspot butterfly, the desert pupfish, the yellow-legged frog, the Galapagos marine iguana, and the bald eagle — but each and every creature and living organism, common or rare, abundant or endangered, and living in any corner of Earth's wild places.

Many friends of nature may not have the time or patience to do everything that a professional naturalist does. We should all know, however, that everyone can find opportunities to experience nature in action, whether on a trip to a National Park or just a walk in the neighborhood. It might involve patient observation, or perhaps just the serendipitous appearance of an animal. All we have to do is pay attention and take delight.

Most of us don't live in wild places. It takes an effort

and a conscience to get out and find and absorb a dose of nature. My adventures happen because I put myself in places where I can be touched by nature, by its simplicity, by its complexity, and by its beauty. As a student and later a professional biologist, I was trying to carry out projects, to collect data, to test hypotheses, to apply for and obtain research grants to finance my adventures, mainly thanks to the National Science Foundation. But I have to confess that my ultimate pleasure was just to go out and find places where I could pay attention and find out what would be revealed. In my continued explorations I take pleasure in conjuring up the same naïve expectations of adventure that I felt as a young man. I know that I will always find beauty out there.

Sometimes I think we may worry too much about the unhappy and worsening consequences of our human domination and transformation of Earth's ecosystems and surrounding atmosphere—so much that our guilt and helplessness become an emotional drain. The situation is discouraging in light of governments, public policies, and the variety of issues that seem to consume our society domestically and internationally. Despite the most recent setbacks in the campaign to protect our Earth, we must maintain hope for the future of the planet and for all the species that share it, including our own.

The problem of climate change embodies many of the issues that need to be fixed to assure Earth's healthy future. Whatever we can do—individually and societally, locally and globally—we need to take action that will move our political system. For me, the underlying motivation comes from my love of nature and from the beauty I've seen. That's what I want to protect.

My experience as a graduate student uncovering the

secret connection between the chisel-toothed kangaroo rat and the spiny saltbush remains a delight—and continues to remind me that everything in nature is worthy of our attention. I hope that each of my stories opens a pathway to nature for my readers, perhaps in ways that will lead to societal change.

As I was pulling together the last bits of this collection at the end of summer 2017, I thought to take a couple of days to visit my nearest National Park, Mount Rainier, whose looming glacier-topped mass I see throughout the year from my home in Seattle a hundred miles away. The mountain and its trees, its persisting late-summer flowers, and its creatures were waiting there to remind me of the peace in pristine nature. I visited the oldest and most gigantic trees—cedar, fir, and hemlock—in the wet lowlands at the base of the mountain. I hiked among the slender, ice-worn spires of subalpine fir along timberline meadows. The last golden-mantled ground squirrels, at the edge of the subalpine forest, were readying themselves for hibernation. A kin group of hoary marmots, the larger cousins of the ground squirrels, busied themselves in the meadow with final preparations as well. The soils along the trails, a mile above sea level, were loose and dusty from the heat and wear of July and August. Many people had paid summer visits, and a few more still came now, in September, to attend to the quiet of the approaching turn of seasons. With the transition from pavement to trailhead, urban life's electronic transmissions ceased—a welcome disconnection.

I was impressed with one persistent and predominant adult marmot, who stood proudly, it seemed to me, atop a low embankment just above the trail. Two still-growing juveniles circled, less confidently, around the burrow entrances along the bank. As I watched the big adult, she turned her back toward me and seemed to look into the distance. I lifted up my eyes and was surprised to see that she stood precisely in my line of sight toward the summit of Mount Rainier some two miles above. I felt in that moment as if she and I were gazing in awe at the same great peak. She turned her head to the side, as if looking over her shoulder at me, and then turned back to the mountain. I suppose the big marmot was not actually pondering the distant massif of Rainier's crown as I was. But I took it all in as a shared experience with the marmot, the meadow, and the mountain — a *moment in nature*. Peace.

References and Further Reading

Bailey, V. 1922. Beaver habits, beaver control and possibilities in beaver farming. *United States Department of Agriculture Bulletin* 1078: 1-29.

Bailey, V. 1936. The mammals and life zones of Oregon. *United States Department of Agriculture. North American Fauna* 55: 1-416.

Barbour, M. G., and W. D. Billings, editors. 2000. *North American Terrestrial Vegetation*. Second Edition. Cambridge University Press.

Belkin, D. A. 1961. The running speeds of the lizards *Dipsosaurus dorsalis* and *Callisaurus draconoides*. *Copeia* 1961: 223-224.

Benedict, A. D., and J. K. Gaydos. 2015. *The Salish Sea: Jewel of the Pacific Northwest*. Sasquatch Books.

Cowles, R. B., and C. M. Bogert. 1944. A preliminary study of the thermal requirements of desert reptiles. *Bulletin of the American Museum of Natural History* 83: 261-296.

Cowles, R. B. 1977. *Desert Journal. A Naturalist Reflects on Arid California*. University of California Press.

Dierenfeld, E., H., et al. 1982. Utilization of bamboo by the giant panda. *Journal of Nutrition* 112: 636-641.

Feldhamer, G. A., et al. 2015. *Mammalogy. Adaptation, Diversity, Ecology*. Fourth Edition. Johns Hopkins University Press.

Fleischner, T. L., et al. 2017. Teaching biology in the field: importance, challenges, and solutions. *BioScience* 67: 558-567.

GeckoWatch. www.inaturalist.org/projects/geckowatch

Genoways, H. H., and J. H. Brown, editors. 1993. *Biology of the Heteromyidae*. Special Publication No. 10, The American Society of Mammalogists.

Grayson, D. K. 2011. *The Great Basin: a Natural Prehistory*. University of California Press.

Hall, E. R. 1946. *Mammals of Nevada*. University of California Press.

Kardong, K. V. 2015. *Vertebrates: Comparative Anatomy, Function, Evolution*. McGraw-Hill Education.

Kenagy, G. J. 1972. Saltbush leaves: excision of hypersaline tissue by a kangaroo rat. *Science* 178: 1094-1096.

Kenagy, G. J. 1973. Adaptations for leaf eating in the Great Basin kangaroo rat, *Dipodomys microps*. *Oecologia* 12: 383-412.

Kenagy, G. J. 1973. Daily and seasonal patterns of activity and energetics in a heteromyid rodent community. *Ecology* 54: 1201-1219.

Kenagy, G. J., and C. B. Smith. 1973. Radioisotopic measurement of depth and determination of temperatures in burrows of heteromyid rodents. *Proceedings of the Third National Symposium on Radioecology*, pages 265-273.

Kenagy, G. J. 1976. Field observations of male fighting, drumming and copulation in the Great Basin kangaroo rat, *Dipodomys microps*. *Journal of Mammalogy* 57: 781-785.

Kenagy, G. J., and R. D. Stevenson. 1982. Role of body temperature in the seasonality of daily activity in tenebrionid beetles of eastern Washington. *Ecology* 63: 1491-1503.

Kenagy, G. J., and G. A. Bartholomew. 1985. Seasonal reproductive patterns in five coexisting California desert rodent species. *Ecological Monographs* 55: 371-397.

Kenagy, G. J., S. M. Sharbaugh, and K. A. Nagy. 1989. Annual cycle of energy and time expenditure in a golden-mantled ground squirrel population. *Oecologia* 78: 269-282.

Kenagy, G. J., et al. 1990. Energy expenditure during lactation in relation to litter size in free-living golden-mantled ground squirrels. *Journal of Animal Ecology* 59: 73-88.

Liu, J., et al., editors. 2016. *Pandas and People. Coupling Human and Natural Systems for Sustainability.* Oxford University Press.

Lowry, D., et al. 2015. Evaluation of creel survey methods to estimate recreational harvest of surf smelt in Puget Sound, Washington. *North American Journal of Fisheries Management* 35: 403-417.

MacMillen, R. E. 1964. Population ecology, water relations, and social behavior of a southern California semidesert rodent fauna. *University of California Publications in Zoology* 71: 1-66.

Munz, P. A., and D. D. Keck. 1963. *A California Flora.* University of California Press.

Reid, F. A. 2006. *A Field Guide to Mammals of North America North of Mexico.* Fourth Edition. Houghton Mifflin.

Rissing, S. W. 1982. Foraging velocity of seed-harvester ants, *Veromessor pergandei* (Hymenoptera: Formicidae). *Environmental Entomology* 11: 905-907.

Schmidt-Nielsen, K. 1964. *Desert Animals. Physiological Problems of Heat and Water.* Oxford University Press.

Schoenherr, A. A. 2017. *A Natural History of California*. Second Edition. University of California Press.

Shapley H. 1920. Thermokinetics of *Liometopum apiculatum* Mayr. *Proceedings of the National Academy of Sciences (USA)* 6: 204-211.

Sibley, D. A. 2014. *The Sibley Guide to Birds*. Second Edition. Alfred A. Knopf.

Smith, G., editor. 2003. *Sierra East: Edge of the Great Basin*. (California Natural History Guides). University of California Press.

Wilson, E. O. 1984. *Biophilia*. Harvard University Press.

Zhang, J., et al. 2015. Activity patterns of the giant panda (*Ailuropoda melanoleuca*). *Journal of Mammalogy* 96: 1116-1127.

Acknowledgments

Many friends and colleagues have kindly advised and encouraged me along the way to writing these stories and putting together this collection. I am enormously thankful to all of them. Special thanks to my recent writing mentors John Elder, Gregory Martin, and Scott Sanders for opening new doors to me. My English teachers Mr. Jones and Mrs. Ferguson pointed the way toward creative writing. Annie Dillard, Brian Doyle, and Ed Abbey provided me with great inspirations.

To Beth Bevis, Anna Blair, Kathryn Flinn, Bernd Heinrich, Tyler McCabe, David McCracken, Susan Mooney, Amy Muia, Steven Otfinoski, Morgan Perlman, Katie Powers, Whitney Sanford, Lauret Savoy, and Rebecca Warren special thanks for critical reading of individual stories.

To Rebecca Andrews, Robert Brown, Suzanne DeRosier, Robert Espinoza, Teresa Horton, Don Hoyt, Ray Huey, Ian Hume, David Kenagy, David Koch, Richard MacMillen, Justin McCarthy, Joshua Mitchell, James Nason, Steven Rissing, Susan Sharbaugh, Jan Smith, Julie Stein, and Robert Stevenson my thanks for sharing reminiscences and information.

To Nancy Smith my appreciation for producing the chapter-head sketches.

I am pleased to acknowledge Richard E. MacMillen of Pomona College and University of California, Irvine, for his mentorship and lasting friendship, and I happily dedicate Chapters 7 and 8 to him.

For permission to quote from Edward O. Wilson's *Biophilia* I thank Harvard University Press, Cambridge, Mass., Harvard University Press, copyright © 1984 by the President and Fellows of Harvard College.

To the National Science Foundation my extreme gratitude for consistent financial support of my scientific career.

Finally to Nancy Kenagy, Mary Kenagy Mitchell, and Craig Smith my greatest thanks for support and encouragement of every kind in the production of this book.

About the Author

Immersed in nature over a lifetime along the Pacific Coast, George James Kenagy was born in California, grew up in Oregon, and completed his education in California. His academic career began in 1976 at the University of Washington, where he continues, since 2008, as emeritus professor of biology and curator of mammals at the Burke Museum of Natural History and Culture. His research spans ecology, physiology, behavior, and evolutionary biology, and he has taught natural history of mammals, environmental physiology, vertebrate zoology, and biogeography. Kenagy studied at Pomona College and the University of California, Los Angeles, followed by post-doctoral experiences at the Max Planck Institut für Verhaltensphysiologie and the University of California, Los Angeles and San Diego campuses. He has recently taken up writing essays that relate his personal experiences in nature over the course of his life. He lives in Seattle and the San Juan Islands and travels most frequently to Latin America.

About the Font

Palatino was designed by Hermann Zapf and initially released in 1949 by the Stempel AG typefoundry in Germany. It is named after Giambattista Palatino, a master calligrapher and contemporary of Leonardo da Vinci, and utilizes classic Italian Renaissance forms.

29853094R00144

Made in the USA
San Bernardino, CA
19 March 2019